CONCILIUM

concilium 1999/4

FAITH IN A SOCIETY OF INSTANT GRATIFICATION

Edited by

Maureen Junker-Kenny
and Miklós Tomka

SCM Press · London
Orbis Books · Maryknoll

Published by SCM Press Ltd, 9–17 St Albans Place, London N1
and by Orbis Books, Maryknoll, NY 10545

ISBN: 0 334 03055 2 (UK)
ISBN: 1 57075 228 1 (USA)

Typeset at The Spartan Press Ltd, Lymington, Hants
Printed by Biddles Ltd, Guildford and King's Lynn

Concilium Published February, April, June, October, December.

Contents

Introduction: Faith in an Experience Society   vii
   MAUREEN JUNKER-KENNY

I · Societies of Instant Gratification in Different Cultures   I

Europe and North America   3
   ZYGMUNT BAUMAN

Asia   10
   JOHN JOSEPH PUTHENKALAM

Latin America at the Turn of the Millennium: Between
   Immediatism and Holiness   16
   MARIA CLARA LUCCHETTI BINGEMER

II · Sociological Analysis   23

Individualism, A Change in Values, The Experience Society:
   Converging Trends in Sociology   25
   MIKLÓS TOMKA

III · Theological Interpretations   37

The Dangerous Memory of Jesus Christ in a Post-Traditional
   Society   39
   ALBERTO MOREIRA

Instant Gratification and Liberation   49
   FERDINAND DAGMANG

The River and the Mountain   59
   SUBHASH ANAND

Aesthetic Existence and Christian Identity   68
   MICHAEL BONGARDT

IV · Ecclesial Praxis: Challenges, Opportunities, Models   79

Decline or Transformation of Solidarity?   81
   NORBERT METTE

New Affective Communities and the Problem of Mutual
   Understanding   91
   DIANA L. HAYES

Fulfilment – Experienced for a Moment yet Painfully Lacking?   101
   HANS KESSLER

Documentation: The Success of 'The Experience Society'
   and the Most Obvious Mistakes in its Reception   113
   GÖTZ LECHNER

Contributors   123

Introduction: Faith in an Experience Society

What power of transformation and resistance is offered by Christian faith in a cultural situation characterized by words like globalization, differentiation, individualization and an orientation on experience? In a social and cultural development which is constantly accelerating, traditional techniques and patterns of behaviour are quickly superseded; historical memory is relativized; and it becomes increasingly difficult to calculate and plan one's own future and that of society. There is increasing pressure to expect everything from the moment and to withdraw into smaller areas which one has chosen for oneself.

Can such an increasing orientation on experience be noted in different continents and cultural spheres, or is it a limited regional phenomenon, typical of the 'First' World which is so dominated by consumerism, as the sociologist Gerhard Schulze has demonstrated in connection with Germany? What place is Schulze's thesis to be given in the history of sociology? The contributions in Parts I and II of this issue pursue these questions. They discuss what contemporary conditions are indicated for bringing about and renewing belief in God. Part III attempts to offer a theological interpretation of the change towards an orientation on experience which is predominantly aesthetic and subjective, in the light of various contexts of inculturation and theological approaches. Can it provide opportunities for new life and immediacy in the experience of God? What obstacles does it put in the way of a faith founded on history, which is orientated on a more than immanent eschatology? Part IV takes up problem areas of the cultural shifts which have been diagnosed, considering their significance for church action: the future of an orientation in solidarity on the common good, the reduction of society to enclaves of feeling relevant to individuals, and the tension between fulfilment, disappointment and a longing for something 'More' and 'Other' which cannot be superseded. The 'documentation' returns to the initial hypothesis of the 'experience society', and by means of its reception by German-speaking sociologists indicates which conclusions are erroneous, which take us further, and which questions remain open.

The proposal to take an orientation on experience as a starting point for the attempt to identify conditions of believing in late modernity and to assess them theologically is open to points of attack which can easily be anticipated: an originally German, provincial, analysis is elevated to become the global key to an interpretation of the present despite all the time-lags and world-wide injustices in the opportunities for survival and experience. Moreover it proved impossible to include three articles: a cultural and theological assessment from an African perspective, a historical analysis of the change to an experience society which is claimed to be happening, and an evaluation of the shift towards the aesthetic in the church's use of symbols. However, the contributions which are included offer a spectrum of questions to be pursued further. Do we have a change fixed on consumerism and possessions or a 'post-materialist' change in which a readiness for doing without and empathy are conceivable attitudes? Does it further the privatization of belief or does it make belief more sensitive to social conditions? How are we to understand trusting faith or belief in a loving and demanding God if structural factors which we ourselves have not chosen lead to the increasing emergence of the self as a precarious point for the construction of a world which is constantly reformed by decisions which can be gone back on? Is the potential of faith called on to resist or to make a cultural synthesis?

It is the task of a theology orientated on praxis to ascertain the relevance of Christian faith for salvation in the face of Christian faith and to work out forms and structures of communication which reach those being addressed. In order to do that, it must take seriously the forms of religion that it encounters as a hermeneutical horizon for the present-day state of the question of meaning. Its present form is also governed by factors like a break in the tradition and the disappearance of the capacity to put oneself and one's time in a historical context. That situation arises as the result of post-modern doubt in the so-called 'grand narratives' with a promise of salvation, the loss of meaning in existing references to society, and the shift from the pole of eschatological hope to the immanence of 'paradise now'. However, those who are put in question are not only contemporary individuals and tendencies with a hunger for experience, but also the churches. The qualities of meaning in the experience society can remind them of what they must be at their very heart: places of symbolic experience for mediating the infinite in the finite, for which there is no secular equivalent.

No analytical conclusion can match the aesthetic tendency of the theme. So instead, here the expressive poetry of Wislawa Szymborska, a

Polish winner of the Nobel Prize for Literature, can attest to constitutive experiences of humanity which need also to be made good in an experience society committed to the 'project of the beautiful life'.

Contribution to statistics

Of one hundred people

— there are fifty-two
who know it all better;

for almost all the rest
every step is uncertain;

those ready to help,
as long as it doesn't take too long,
— as many as forty-nine;

those always gracious,
because they cannot change anything,
— four, perhaps five;

those led astray by youth,
the transitory,
— plus or minus sixty;

those who will not tolerate any jokes,
who have a talent to be happy
— rather more than twenty, at most;

those who are wise after the event
— not many more
than those who are wise before the event;

those bowed down, tested by suffering,
without a lamp in the dark
— eighty-three, sooner or later;

the upright
— a great many, say thirty-five;

if this characteristic coincides
with the effort to understand
— three;

those worthy of compassion
– ninety-nine;

The mortal
one hundred per cent
A number which at present does not change.

Maureen Junker-Kenny
Miklós Tomka

I · Societies of Instant Gratification in Different Cultures

Europe and North America

Zygmunt Bauman

Already the ancients knew the truth. In his dialogue *On a Happy Life*, Lucius Annaeus Seneca pointed out that in stark opposition to the pleasures of virtue, the delights of rapture cool off when at their hottest; their capacity is so small that it fills up to exhaustion in no time. Invigorated but for a fleeting moment, the seekers of sensual pleasure quickly fall into languor and apathy. In other words, their happiness is short-lived and their dreams are self-destructive. Seneca warned: the gratification quickest to come is also one that dies first.

The ancient sage had also guessed what kind of people tend to choose a life dedicated to the search for such pleasures as bring gratification instantly. In another dialogue, *On The Brevity of Life*, he noted that this kind of life was the lot of people who forgot the past, did not care about the present, and were afraid of the future.

True observations about the human predicament stay true for a long time. Their truth is not affected by trials of history. Seneca's insights, no doubt, belong in this category. The endemic frailty of instant gratification and the close link between the obsession of instant delight, indifferent to what has been and the distrust of what is to come, tend to be confirmed today as they were two millennia ago. What has changed are the numbers of people who experience at first hand the misery of living in a flattened and sliced time. What for Seneca seemed to be but a sign of regrettable deviation from the right path – of the way lost and life wasted – has turned into the norm. What used to be a choice of the few is now the fate of the many. In order to understand why this has happened, we could do worse than follow Seneca's hunches.

The title of a paper given in December 1997 by one of the most perceptive social analysts of our times, Pierre Bourdieu, was 'Le précarité est aujourd'hui partout'. The title told it all: precariousness, instability, vulnerability is the most widespread (as well as the most painfully felt) feature of contemporary life. The French theorists speak of *précarité*, the German of *Unsicherheit* and *Risikogesellschaft*, the Italians of *incertezza* and the English of *insecurity*. All have in mind the same aspect of human predicament, experienced all over the highly developed, modernized and well-off part of the globe, and felt there to be especially unnerving and depressing by reason of being new and in many ways unprecedented. The phenomenon they try to grasp is the combined experience of *insecurity* of position, entitlements and livelihood, of *uncertainty* as to their continuation and future stability, and of *unsafety* of one's body, one's self and their extensions: possessions, neighbourhood, community. Seneca deprecated the tendency to forget the past, not to care about the present, and to fear the future as his contemporaries' personal failings; but we may say today that in our fellow humans' experience, the past does not count for much, since it does not offer secure foundations for life's prospects; the present is not given proper care since it is virtually out of control; and there are good reasons to be afraid that the future has further unpleasant surprises, trials and tribulations in store. Nowadays, precariousness is not a matter of choice; it is fate.

To have faith means to have trust in the meaning of life and to expect long-lasting importance of what one does or desists from doing. Faith comes easy when experience confirms that this trust is well founded. Only in a relatively stable world, in which things and acts retain their value over a long period of time, a period commensurate with the length of human life, is such confirmation likely to be offered. In a logical and consistent world human actions also acquire logic and consistency. Living in such a world, as the eminent ethical philosopher Hans Jonas put it, we count days and the days count. Our times are hard for faith – *any* faith, sacred or secular; for belief in Providence, the Divine Chain of Being, as much as for belief in a mundane utopia, in a perfect society to come. Our times are inhospitable for trust, and more generally for the long-haul purposes and efforts, because of the evident transience and vulnerability of everything (or almost everything) that counts in earthly life.

To start with the preliminary condition for all the rest: our livelihood. This has become exceedingly fragile. German economists write of the '*zwei-Drittel Gesellschaft*' and expect it to become soon an '*ein-Drittel*' one, meaning that everything needed to satisfy the market demand can be produced now by two-thirds of the population, and soon one-third will be enough – leaving other men and women without employment, making them *economically* useless and *socially* redundant. However brave the faces politicians make and however audacious their promises, unemployment in the affluent countries has become 'structural': there is simply not enough work for everybody.

How brittle and uncertain the life of those directly affected has become in the result does not take much imagination to adumbrate. The point is, though, that everybody else is also affected, if for the time being indirectly. In the world of structural unemployment, no one can feel secure. There is no such thing as secure jobs in secure companies any more; nor are there many skills and experiences which, once acquired, guarantee that a job will be offered and, once offered, will be lasting. No one may reasonably assume to be insured against the next round of 'downsizing', 'streamlining' or 'rationalizing', against erratic shifts of market demand and whimsical yet powerful pressures of 'competitiveness' and 'effectiveness'. 'Flexibility' is the catchword of the day. It augurs jobs without in-built security of entitlements: fixed-term or rolling contracts, dismissal without notice and compensation.

No one can feel truly irreplaceable; even the most privileged position may prove to be but temporary and 'until further notice'. And if human beings do not count, nor do the days of their lives. In the absence of long-term security, 'instant gratification' looks enticingly like a reasonable strategy. Whatever life may offer, let it offer it *hic et nunc* – right away. Who knows what tomorrow may bring? Delay of satisfaction has lost its allure: it is, after all, highly uncertain whether the labour and effort invested today will count as assets by the time it takes to reach reward; it is far from certain, moreover, that the prizes which look attractive today will be still desirable when at long last they come. Assets tend to become liabilities, glittering prizes turn into badges of shame, fashions come and go with mind-boggling speed, all objects of desire become obsolete and off-putting before they have time to be fully enjoyed. Styles of life which are 'chic' today will tomorrow become targets of ridicule.

If this is the case, then to avoid frustration one had better refrain from developing habits and attachments or entering lasting commitments. The objects of desire are better enjoyed on the spot and then disposed of; markets see to it that they are made in such a way that both the gratification and the obsoleteness are instant. Not just the contents of the wardrobe need to be changed every season: cars need to be replaced because their body design has become old-fashioned and hurts the eye; good computers are thrown on the scrapheap because new gadgets made them out-of-date; splendid and cherished music collections on LPs are replaced by cassettes, only to be replaced again by CDs simply because new recordings are no longer available in previous forms.

Men and women are thereby trained (made to learn the hard way) to perceive the world as a container full of disposable objects, objects for one-off use. The whole world – including other human beings. Every item is replaceable, and had better be replaceable: what if greener grass appears, if better – yet untried – joys beckon from afar? In a world in which the future is full of dangers, any chance not taken here and now is a chance missed; not taking it is thus unforgivable and cannot be justified. Since present-day commitments stand in the way of next-day opportunities, the lighter and more superficial they are, the less the damage. 'Now' is the keyword of life strategy, whatever that strategy may refer to. Through an insecure and unpredictable world, smart and clever wanderers travel light, and shed no tears for anything that cramped the moves.

And so the policy of 'precarization' conducted by the operators of labour markets is aided and abetted by life policies. Both converge on the same result: the fading and wilting, falling apart and decomposing of human bonds, communities and partnerships. Commitments of the 'till death us do part' type become contracts 'until satisfaction lasts', temporal by definition and design – and amenable to being broken unilaterally, whenever one of the partners sniffs better value in opting out rather than continuing the relationship.

In other words, bonds and partnerships are viewed as things to be *consumed*, not produced; they are subject to the same criteria of evaluation as all other objects of consumption. In the consumer market, the ostensibly durable products are as a rule offered for a 'trial period', and money back is promised if the purchaser is less than fully satisfied. If the partner in partnership is seen in these terms, then it is no longer the task of both partners to 'make the relationship work' – to see it work through thin and thick, to help each other through good and bad patches, to trim one's own preferences if need be, to compromise and make sacrifices for the sake of lasting union. Instead it is a matter of obtaining satisfaction from a ready-to-use product: if the pleasure derived is not up to the standard promised and expected, or if the novelty wears off together with the joy, there is no reason to stick to the inferior or aged product rather than find another, 'new and improved' one, in the shop.

What follows is that the assumed temporariness of partnerships tends to turn into a self-fulfilling prophecy. If the human bond, like all other consumer objects, is not something to be worked out through protracted effort and occasional sacrifice, but something which one expects to bring satisfaction right away, that one rejects if it does not, and keeps and uses only as long as it continues to gratify (and no longer) – there is not much point in trying harder and harder, let alone in suffering discomfort and unease in order to save the partnership. Even a minor stumble may cause the partnership to come to grief; petty disagreements turn into bitter conflicts; slight frictions are taken to signal essential incompatibility. As the American sociologist W. I. Thomas would say: if people assume their commitments to be temporary and until further notice, these commitments do tend to become like that in consequence of people's own actions.

In these times of uncertainty and precariousness, transience acquires a 'strategic edge' over durability. It is no longer clear what is the cause and what is the effect. Is the fragility and vulnerability of the human condition the summary result of common-life policies that do not recognize long-term purposes and values which are hard to earn and preserve? Or is it rather that people tend to prefer short-term satisfaction because little in the world is truly durable and few objectives may be relied upon to outlive the effort needed to fulfil them? Both suppositions are partly true and each conveys a part of truth. The world saturated with uncertainty, and lives sliced into short-lived episodes required to bring instant gratification aid and abet, support and reinforce each other.

A crucial part of any faith is the investment of value in something more durable than the evanescent and endemically mortal individual life: something lasting, resistant to the eroding impact of time, perhaps even immortal and eternal. Individual death is unavoidable, but life may be used to negotiate and earn a place in eternity. Life may be lived in such a fashion that individual mortality is transcended, so that the trace left by life is not completely effaced. Faith may be a spiritual matter, but in order to hold it needs mundane anchoring; its roots must reach deep into the experience of daily life.

For a long time family served as one of the principal links connecting mortal beings to immortality: individual life leads to lasting values. Yellowing photographs in family albums, and before that the long lists of birth, wedding and funeral dates in family Bibles, testified to the longevity of the family, which individual members should do nothing to jeopardize and everything to make secure. Family albums, though, have now been replaced by camcorders with video-cassettes, and video tapes differ from photographic paper in being eminently effaceable. They are meant to be effaced again and again to make room for new, similarly temporary, recordings. The substitution of videos for photographs has symbolic significance; it fits the changing status of family life, which for a growing number of men and women has now become an event not necessarily longer-lasting than individual life. Families tend to be made and unmade a number of times during the life-span of a single individual. The family can hardly serve as a material, solid and reliable bridge to immortality.

However enormous the consequences of this development are, they are not alone; what happens nowadays to the family mirrors profound changes taking place in the other aspects of the human condition, which once upon a time provided bridges leading from individual mortality to durable, even immortal, values. One may say that immortality itself tends to become 'instant'. One can hear the broadcasters of sporting events or pop-music festivals announcing, in voices choked with excitement, that they (and the viewers) are 'witnessing history being made'. In its new rendition, immortality is not something to be earned the hard way, through lifelong effort; it is, rather, something to be enjoyed on the spot, without giving much thought to the consequences – without asking how really eternal that instantly-relished 'immortality' will prove to be. Artists used to take the greatest care to assure the durability of their murals and canvases, architects used to erect buildings meant to last for centuries to come. Now, the favourite art materials are those that brandish and flaunt their perishability: a favourite form of visual art is the 'happening' or installation, patched together as a one-off event, for the duration of an exhibition, and destined to be dismantled the night after the gallery closes. In all fields of culture (including science – allegedly concerned with eternal truths), notoriety replaces fame; and notoriety is, admittedly and unashamedly, the instant version of immortality, oblivious and indifferent to all other versions.

If dedication to lasting values is in crisis today, it is because the very idea of duration, of immortality, is in crisis too. But immortality is in crisis because the basic, daily trust in the durability of things towards which and by which human life may be orientated is undermined by daily human experience. That erosion of trust is, in turn, perpetrated by the endemic precariousness, fragility, insecurity and uncertainty of the human place in human society.

The promotion of competitiveness, and of a 'free-for-all' pursuit of the highest gain, to the rank of the superior (even monopolistic) criterion in distinguishing between proper and improper, right and wrong action, is the factor bearing the ultimate responsibility for the 'ambient fear' –

which permeates the contemporary life of most men and women and their widespread feeling of insecurity, which is perhaps universally shared. Society no longer guarantees, nor even promises, a collective remedy for individual misfortunes. Individuals have been offered (or, rather, have been cast in) freedom of unprecedented proportions – but at the price of similarly unprecedented insecurity. And when there is insecurity, little time is left for the care in values that hover above the level of daily concerns – or, for that matter, for whatever lasts longer than the fleeting moment.

Fragmented life tends to be lived in episodes, in a series of unconnected events. Insecurity is a point at which being breaks down into fragments, and life into episodes. Unless something is done about the haunting spectre of insecurity, the restoration of faith in values lasting and durable stands little chance.

Asia

John Joseph Puthenkalam

The composition of place or cultural setting

The ideas that are borne out of our minds are materialized as human realities in and through our personal lives. Our lives, especially our modern/post-modern lives, are interdisciplinary in nature. The mega-trends that unfold with the rising and setting of the sun are incomprehensible to our cellular but brilliant minds. Our new age which demands more political freedoms and more economic development and more respect for cultures is in fact resulting in the evolution of a new global economic order: globalization. Though it is mostly understood (popularly) in terms of economics, many other socio-political and religio-cultural factors play a role. This article is an attempt to introduce a few premises for the Asian context, which, if integrated into our theological dialogue, would enhance the opportunities for a new immediacy of God-relatedness in our intimations of Christian faith. I would like to begin with a philosophical question. Does the way of thinking (culture, philosophy plus theology) of a particular nation or region enable one to explore the potential and the problem that a society of instant gratification poses for mediating the Christian message? To ask this is to question the culture. The new awareness that we derive from this process of questioning would inevitably lead us to the deeper implications of the relevance of the Asian church today.

Since the beginning of civilization, we have been in pursuit of taming nature. In a broad sense, this human act is the first instance of what is now termed 'instant gratification'. Humans have been able to tame nature to their satisfaction. As the process of civilization has been conscientized, the spirit of the human being has emerged, to be called culture. The moment the human agent becomes aware of the culture in which he or she is situated, he or she also turns out to be an agent who develops and remoulds the culture. The way of thinking that exists in the micro-agent expands and spreads into the macro-level. The outcome is the birth of a culture, a national philosophy, which penetrates into every corner of the whole nation and its every action. Every nation needs to become aware of the existing way of thinking that motivates its people to act. To a great extent, it is this awareness that brings change, and in the economic sphere, this conscientized change is termed economic development. Whether they live in developed or developing economies, people want to have an instant share of this developmental cake. A society of instant gratification is being born. The result of this process of instant gratification is the phenomenon of 'rural-push' and 'urban-pull'. This phenomenon caused the problem of the mega-cities where everyone gathers, where everything is produced and where new rich are being designed and built into empires of admiration. Asia is an example of this new trend, that has challenged its traditions and life-style and value-systems.

The Asian scenario

The Asian region is characterized by extraordinary contradictions and paradoxes. Certainly one of the most beautiful regions on the planet, and rich in resources, in recent decades Asia's social landscape has become marred by recurrent intra-regional wars and civil conflicts, chronic human rights violations, corrupt governments, and growing poverty (World Bank, 1990; UNDP, 1994 and 1997). Population growth continues to be one of the most rapid in the world, as is the region's rate of urban migration (UN, 1989). In recent years, the economic crisis has deepened and would thwart most of its achievement.[1] This is the context of the Asian church today.

For the universal Catholic Church, while the years since Vatican II are considered as the remote preparatory days towards the third millennium, the three years from 1997 are considered as imminent preparatory days towards The Great Jubilee Year. In union with the spirit of these years, the Synod for Asia, along with the other synods, we hope, is an attempt to prepare itself to respond to the demands of this coming millennium. 'The Coming of the Third Millennium' has significant implications for the church in Asia. Already, the secular-material world has seen and acknowledged the emergence of the Asia–Pacific region as a regional block to be reckoned with in the global scene. The emergence of the Asia–Pacific region brings in new challenges for the church in the Asia–Pacific region. Translating the 'vision-mission' statements of the Federa-

tion of Asian Bishops Conference (FABC) on the eve of a new
millennium invites us to look at the new realities that are unfolding
before us and thus thematize the relevance and contribution the church
in Asia can make.

These new realities with their gentleness as well as with their
determinedness touch our small personal lives along with the throbbing
of the larger society in which we consummate our lives. What are those
new realities . . . have we noticed their arrival . . . do we notice their
power . . . who are the players – the decision-makers, the beneficiaries or
the victims? If we do not recognize those new realities with all their
meanings and meaninglessness, we are away from reading the 'signs of
the times'. If we recognize those new realities and do not grasp them, we
are away from analysis and understanding. Our response to a situation
simply depends on our understanding of this real situation. Therefore,
we may ask: 'What experiences of immediacy, gratification or fulfilment
can the Christian religion offer in the midst of a consumer society that
tends to exclude the needy?' Traditional Asia used to be contemplative in
her essence, but modern Asia is dynamic and active and apostolic. The
church in Asia could integrate these traditional and modern characteristics in her desire to relate to all people of God in Asia. This is possible
by 'experiencing society' as it unfolds in the Asian soil. I begin by a
meditation with the cosmic Christ whom we as an Asian church want to
proclaim.

Who do you say that I am?

How do the Asians and particularly the Christians in Asia respond to this
query of Christ? While Yahweh and Brahman and Allah 'is' One for all
peoples of Asia, how do we explain to our contemporaries the revelation
of Yahweh alone in Jesus Christ? While the Holy Bible and the Bhagavad
Gita and the Holy Quran 'are' sacred books for all peoples of Asia, how
do we explain to our contemporaries the Bible and its good news? While
the minority of Christians and the majority of Hindus, Buddhists and
Muslims in Asia worship the Eternal God in all divine splendour, it
would be worthy to emphasize the similarity rather than the difference. If
we emphasize the similarity, it would promote mutual respect and intra-
inter-religious dialogue which we urgently need in Asia. If we emphasize
the difference, there is a high incidence of probability that it would lead
to ethnic and religious fundamentalism which would retard the Asianness and the Asian values that we have developed through the previous

millennia. Through the millennia, we have harmoniously lived as Christian-Hindu-Buddhist-Muslim brothers and sisters. I would like to confess Jesus as the Christ, the Son of the Living God, with all the church's apostolic traditions and teachings in Asia, without fear or prejudice to other religious faiths and their traditions and teachings. This fearless profession of faith in Jesus Christ is the core and essence of the minority Christians in Asia and the base for the continuity of the apostolic works of the church in Asia. This profession of faith calls for a faith beyond instant gratification.

Who do you say that the church is?

This is an Asian question. We speak here very specifically of the Catholic Church in Asia. As we gather for worship among the thousands of ancient and traditional temples and shrines and mosques and churches we find ourselves and our identity as the Asian people of God. What is a temple or a shrine or a mosque to a person who goes to church? What does a church mean to a person going to a temple or a shrine or a mosque? This interrelated question has to be understood not just in its transcendental nature alone, but also in its existential characteristic. More than a mere institutional expression of a group of religious faithful, should this institutional structure mediate anything in this living dynamic world of ours? If we say 'yes', we can look at our church and ask what this mediation should involve for her life to be meaningful and understood in her local/national/and international milieu. What does the physical presence of the church evoke in her contemporaries in Asia? Do people feel that the church is journeying and sharing in their day-to-day joys and sorrows? To a great extent we can be affirmative in saying that we are theoretically there. Our institutions, the external visible signs of the presence of the church in the world, are at the service of the local and national needs. Our educational institutions, our hospitals and health-care network, our pastoral and socio-cultural centres, etc. through a progressive internal conscientization deepen their commitment to work for the promotion of faith and justice. Yet we feel our own inadequacies to respond to the socio-political and economic demands the modern Asian world expects from us and this makes us existentially minimal. Yet, our ongoing Christian commitment calls for a faith beyond instant gratification.

Do we notice the megatrends of the secular Asia?

An analysis of the social-political and economic indices would show the church's minimal presence and inadequate representation in any of the major areas of policy-making in secular Asia. In a sense, the church is not able to be there to influence the major secular trends that affect the lives of the billions of people of Asia. As I have already noted, socially we are a minority except in the Philippines. The Asian church's social strength lies in its international character and in its desire to be with the outcast of the society wherever they are. Our political votes do not determine the formation of any national government. The Asian church's political strength lies in its gospel-oriented apolitically correct FABC documents and its effort at implementation in local and regional churches. Our commitment to uphold the dignity of the human person and assure his or her human rights in spite of the various forms of oppression and violence is in the right direction. The emerging awareness of women's role within the church and in society is to be promoted if we really want to bring about a social equality of status between man and woman.

Our region's Christian economic market is too small to be noted by any capitalist entrepreneur. No market would collapse in Asia because of a decision by the hierarchical church in Asia. The effects of the General Agreement on Trade and Tariff (GATT), the trends of the process of globalization, the media explosion, etc., are to be seen in our context and analysed. The Asian church's economic strength lies in its being a church of the poor, who constitute the majority in this region. This is the reality and the powerlessness of the church in Asia. Even in the face of such powerlessness and minimal presence, we need to be aware of the negative and positive effects of the major developments and megatrends in Asia so that we can be effective instruments of transition to a better world. It is in this emerging trend that we confront a consumer society which is all for instant gratification. In this competitive race for survival we tend to exclude the needy. It is by including the excluded and by embracing the marginalized that the Asian church witnesses to Jesus Christ and his gospel. This calls for a faith which is contrary to the instant gratification faith of the modern consumer society.

Conclusion

The maturity and wisdom of Asia is being tested in the crucible of Asian socio-economic and religio-cultural realities. The Asianness of the Asian church will determine its continuing relevance in our region. In order to be a relevant and prophetic witness to the gospel of Jesus Christ through the Asian church among all the peoples of Asia, we need to develop a praxis-orientated analysis of the realities of Asia. I hope that the above integrated analysis of the Asian reality and the Asian church will enable many pastoral agents to design approaches and directives to read and respond to the signs of the times in their own wounded yet redeemed situations. As we endeavour to design a new vision-mission strategy out of the Asian reality that we have seen already, as well as the unfolding new realities of everyday life, let us unite with the mystics and martyrs and saints of the Asian church, and pray to the Lord of the Universe that 'Thy will be done on this Asian earth as in the heavens', in all ages to come.

Note

1. The region's clearest expressions of its development priorities are outlined in ESCAP (1992), *Social Development Strategy for the ESCAP Region Towards the Year 2000 and Beyond*, and ESCAP (1988), *The Jakarta Plan of Action on Human Resources Development*.

Latin America at the Turn of the Millennium: Between Immediatism and Holiness

Maria Clara Lucchetti Bingemer

In Brazil today, as in many other parts of the modern Western world, which thought itself free of the oppression and 'opium' of religion, there is a new and intensely powerful explosion of the seductive force of the sacred and the divine, de-repressed and uncontrollable.[1] This is the phenomenon of the so-called 'sects' or alternative religious groups, which fill the religious field with new and disconcerting forms of expression, frightening as well as intriguing the traditional historical churches, social scientists and intelligentsia.[2]

It is a documented fact that millions of Brazilians go into a trance every day: that is, they are torn out of their willed and affective potential by some experience of the Transcendent, identified with the sacred or the holy, whether this is called God, Oxalá or St Damian.[3] Behind this complex and plural religious explosion there lurk, it seems to me, questions of the utmost importance not only for theology but for all the social and human sciences that seek to engage seriously with this more-than-human problem of religious experience or experience of the sacred.

From one angle, they pose a veiled criticism of the traditional historical churches, which seem to have lost much of their initiating, mysterious character, remaining characterized virtually by their institutional aspect alone – formational for the community, or bringing ethics to bear in order to change society. In connection with this, the effort being made within the bosom of institutionalized Christianity itself to use techniques of the oriental traditions as an aid to spiritual experience can be seen as a way or an attempt to recover initiating and mystagogical Christianity. We are also witnessing the frightening advance of New Age movements, of Pentecostalist sects, and – within the historical churches – of the charismatic movement.[4]

Is this a crisis of modernity or of its paradigms?

The paradigm of modernity – though still all too healthy and vigorous in some ways – is giving clear signs of at least partial weakening, of crisis. The ideology of progress is being deeply questioned. The social, political and economic systems that have devoted the best part of their energies to propounding this ideology do not seem to have made a very good job of it, at least in regard to the great questions of the meaning of existence and the purpose of life, which still disturb hearts and minds.

In Latin America the largest economies (Brazil, Argentina and Chile) are arguing about the need to find a place in the ranks of the great capitalist powers, while sinking ever deeper into the deceptive depths of a system that drags them into a spiral of debt that penalizes the poorest classes and destroys the viability of social progress for these countries.

Allied to this state of affairs, to this sort of more or less generalized 'disorientation', is no less disorientation in relation to utopias, ways of thinking, political models and other matters. People, at the same time as they find themselves in a chaotic situation with regard to the actual administration of their resources and the organization of their economic, political and social systems, are seeking rapid escapes and immediate gratifications outside their material existence. This is perhaps the main reason for the subject of mysticism being 'in' and such a debating-point among so many different groups.

The resacralization of the very world whose dis-enchantment and secularism modern reasoning was so quick to proclaim complicates these questions. The reappearance or re-emergence – more than once – of the religious, of the sacred, of thirst for mystery and mysticism in various forms comes after their supposed 'banishment' by secularization. While this wild religiosity is symptomatic of a lack and of a disordered and uncontrolled need, it can have its positive side, in that it represents a return (if not the permanence) of the need for contemplation, an apparently new emergence of values such as gratuitousness, desire, feelings and the rediscovery, in a new dimension, of nature and our relationship with the planet.

We still need to ask whether one thing is the consequence of the other: whether, that is, for mysticism and contemplation to be 'in' and become subjects of prime concern, it is necessary for everything that forms the world of doing and acting, of transforming efficacy, of conscious and articulated intervention, to be 'out' or to have obviously failed. In other words, whether to enter fully into the world of mysticism we have to become disenchanted with and renounce politics or policy-making, to desist from long-term planning. Or vice-versa: we need to question whether opting for life in the *polis*, in the world, in the secular city, means turning our back on mysticism, which would then be fated to become the business of a few specialist inhabitants of cloisters and monasteries or of other types of explicitly contemplative religious communities.

It is at least instructive to discover that this is happening in a world that had, on the contrary, canonized praxis as the *locus* of human and historical self-understanding. The modern world made praxis its central characteristic and converted it into pragmatism. What cannot be turned into action has no value; only what is effective is valid; truth is immediately 'practicable'. In terms of knowledge and learning, it is equally true that only what can be put into practice, what is useful, is valued. Knowledge, therefore, is being able to take hold of objects, generating a praxis of domination and lordship. Applied to politics, efficacy is the great yardstick, putting strategy ahead of people and the common good – regarding people, in the final analysis, as links in the chain that pulls in material goods and power relationships.

The need for an overall ethical view

The greater part of academic studies of the context in which we live today run a serious and obvious risk from the very fact that they are produced from within the belly of the phenomenon known as the crisis of modernity, which tends to sectionalize and fragment events and symptoms and to address them from a monographic standpoint – in sociological or cultural terms, for instance. In other words, they can lead to a unilateral reduction of the complexity and a resultant deformation of the many-sided texture of reality. The diagnoses of the crisis in which we as the Western world – and in our particular case, that of Brazil, of Latin America, a country and a continent in the half of the world that is suffering the consequences of being victimized by the modern process – are immersed do not seem to have helped to solve much.

Our societies are characterized by an abundance of means and a shortage of ends. Never have the means at people's disposition been so abundant and so sophisticated as they are now. And never, perhaps, has it been so obvious that people have lost the ultimate meaning of their lives and destinies from view, contenting themselves with remaining atrophied, reduced to spending their energies and their lives on the quest for immediate and transitory gratifications – as fragile, therefore, as can be.

It is an undoubted fact that conventional ethical models, in the socio-cultural ambits in which modernity has implanted itself and rules, or in which it has tried to impose itself, tend to wither and disappear, at least relatively. On the other hand, where modernity has not shown itself, or has shown itself in a manner and synthesis different from those of the countries called modern, or again in those countries or places from which it appears to be beating retreat,[5] the conventional models are not only not disappearing but are even consolidating themselves. And there is no doubt that the process of changing utopias and paradigms that we are going through today, which implies the demystification of the collective paradigm that 'real socialism' seemed to bring with it, is leading us to rethink the pertinence of a return of an ethical model based on individual and situation ethics.[6]

The lack of clearly defined referential models, constructed around personal values and envisaging specific and identifiable situations, has brought about – in my view – a certain 'ethical nebulousness' in which individuals and groups are groping about at this turn of the millennium. Wandering lost in search of terms of reference to give them solidity in the chaos through which they move and the identification they desperately want, people today are as it were chained to a weak 'ethos' that is losing maturity instead of acquiring it. In their desperate attempt to free themselves from previously established parameters, they actually often find a many-sidedness that frequently leads them to moral weakening and an insecurity and indeterminacy that finally lead them into an attitude which, while trumpeting total freedom from conventional morality, in fact reintroduces shocking habits of rigidity and intolerance.[7]

The continent of Latin America would seem to offer most elements for tracing an outline, however incomplete, of the eventuality indicated above, of the existence of human beings capable of demonstrating an absolute ethical radicalness stemming from or motivated by an experience of faith.[8] I start from the presupposition that Christianity has been a relevant factor in the history of Western civilization, to the point that this presented itself as 'Christian civilization' over a long period of time. This civilization was then exported through expansionist colonial endeavours to various other points of the planet, among which we Latin Americans sadly take our place. This, though, does not invalidate the problematic and pressing nature of the question but rather increases it.[9] It increases it because it prompts further questions. Has the historical impact of Christianity in the West been ethical and humanizing or not? Can we still find humanizing and renewing elements for an ethic in the Christian event? Does Christianity today still have chances of offering ethical models to the men and women of Latin America who have been put through the later sieves of modernity or – ill or well called – postmodernity?

Rediscovery of gratuitousness and otherness?

We are witnessing the dismantling of totalitarian utopianisms and also the weakening of conventional ethical and religious models in the face of the urgent need to regulate our undreamt-of powers of intervention in the world, as cynical and powerful theories advance globally to dominate the lives of dispossessed, marginalized, destitute and suffering people throughout the world. So we need to ask what vision of human beings we have, which will influence the conception we also have of *autos*, of *heteros* and of *nomos*. This in turn leads to examining the possibility of establishing criteria that identify the diverse and diversified experiences that unfold before our eyes as experiences of meaning.

If the ideal, the finality, of the human being, the individual, is 'I' as the same, then the heteronomy and otherness all around us can really be experienced as slavery, as alienation in the face of the other who forces me, oppresses me or alienates me. But if this ideal and finality are different, are building community and establishing relationships of solidarity, of freedom experienced in daily living, then the otherness of others becomes – with all the risks and dangers and conflicts along the way – the condition for making my 'I' possible, something that institutes it, grounds it and allows it to be and exist.

Christianity poses love for the other as a possible road to identifying this 'I'. Loving others as oneself is, already in the Old Testament, the greatest of the commandments, equal in greatness to that of loving God above all things. In the New Testament both together are taken by Jesus as a summary, a happy synthesis of the law and the prophets. In Christianity, human beings are seen as people free to love. Freedom is not conceived as an oppressive heteronomy, in the sense of an external law that crushes and destroys subjectivity, but is the free gift of God who continually sets and re-sets human beings on the way of love, on course towards others. And if Paul states that it is not the law that saves, it is also the same Paul who insists that true freedom lies in loving obedience, provided one understands obedience – the verb *obaudire* means to listen – as practical listening to the instituting, revealing and founding Word of God. Biblical 'man', however, as envisaged by the New Testament, seeing himself free, sees himself, more than anything, as set free: he does not see himself as the source of his own freedom. The source of his autonomy, in this case, lies in a heteronomy: in the other who gratuitously and continually sets him free, writing on the tablets of flesh that are his body – which Paul sets in parallel to the tablets of stone on which the Old Law was inscribed – the law of the new commandment, which is the law of love.

Perhaps the nub of the question – from the Christian viewpoint – lies in an understanding of autonomy and heteronomy as two irreconcilable poles with no possible way out of the impasse. The Christian vision tries to take a step out from this by saying that freedom does not come purely from outside, but is within us, like an inner inscription of the epiphanic challenge, the manifestation of the face that instituted the only law for us, the law of love. And this love is understood not only in terms of a quest for pleasure and satisfaction of instincts and needs, but in those of enticed freedom, of gratuitous self-giving, of self-oblation, in which everything is placed at the service of building a fraternal solidarity, new relationships, a reign of freedom in which even sexual renunciation can have its place, as a choice of freedom in the name of a greater project.

The time in which we live is, then, committed to the problematic recovery of this spiritual sense of *holiness*. In an age so zealous for efficiency, productivity and the usefulness of actions, at a moment in history when the search for instantaneous gratification rules all personal and social organization, turning to 'life stories' means giving a voice to men and women who have apparently 'failed', since they are not preoccupied with efficiency and have given the primacy in their lives to contemplation, from which the practice of charity derives.

This contemplation, in its turn, is not an exercise in generalizing abstraction, but an observation of a definite presence. In other words: there are no saints in the abstract, just specific saints, who are individually empirical. It is not conceptual determination that brings us closer to being saints, nor do the concepts of sociology or history of religion teach us their true essence.[10] Recognition of holiness presupposes a relationship of dialogue with its presence, which – to some extent – requires a *sharing* in its way of life.[11] The endeavour to share in this way is certainly needed if the peoples of Latin America are to be able to resignify their quest for meaning without allowing themselves to be drowned in the intoxication of the search for immediate gratification.

Translated by Paul Burns

Notes

1. On the question of whether we are witnessing a 'return' of the sacred or the religious see, among others, M. França Miranda, 'Volta do sagrado: uma avaliação teológica', *Perspectiva Teológica* 21, 1989, 71–83; id., 'Ser cristão numa sociedade pluralista', ibid., 33–49; L. A. Gomez de Sousa, 'Secularização em declínio e potencialidade transformadora do sagrado', *Religião e sociedade* 132, 1986, 2–16; 'Secularização e sagrado', *Síntese* 13, 1986, 33–9; J. Sudbrack, *La nueva religiosidad. Un desafío para los Cristianos*, Madrid 1990; M. C. Bingemer, *Alteridade e Vulnerabilidade. Experiência de Deus e pluralismo religioso no moderno em crise*, São Paulo 1993.
2. Cf. M. Azevedo, 'Igreja, cultura e libertação', in *Entrocamentos e entrechoques. Vivendo a fé num mundo plural*, São Paulo 1991, 71–4.
3. On this question see R. Otto, *Lo santo. Lo racional y Lo irracional en la idea de Dios*, Madrid 1980, esp. 14–21.
4. As a reaffirmation of the concerns of the Christian churches and, specifically, of the Catholic Church in Brazil for the phenomenon described above, see the recent documents in the 'Studies' collection of the Brazilian Bishops' Conference (CNBB), no. 62, *Igreja católica e pluralismo religioso* (I) and (II).
5. I am thinking here very specifically of the Islamic fundamentalist countries, for example.
6. M. Rubio, 'El contexto de la modernidad y de la postmodernidad', in M. Vidal (ed.), *Conceptos fundamentales de ética teologica*, Madrid 1992, 131.
7. Ibid., 143.
8. In saying this, I am not presuming to exclude the existence of other examples and models of life in other religions or philosophies, but it does seem to me that the Christian typology of holiness can make a specific contribution. In view of this, I have chosen it.
9. On this opening statement see what J. G. Caffarena says in his 'Aportación cristiana a un nuevo humanismo?', in J. Mugueraza, F. Quesada and R. R. Aramayo (eds), *Etica día tras día*, Madrid 1991, 188.
10. See W. Nigg, *Grosse Heilige*, Zurich 1986, 14.
11. For a development of this see M. Buber, *Do diálogo e do dialógico*, São Paulo 1982.

II · Sociological Analysis

Individualism, A Change in Values, The Experience Society: Converging Trends in Sociology

Miklós Tomka

Like the doctrine of predestination, materialist sociology argues for the iron hand of determinism on human existence. Whereas Calvinistic theologians related this to human salvation, Marx asserted that the course of history follows unchangeable given laws. In the former case God was identified as the ultimate cause of the predetermination, in the latter the ultimate cause was the means of production. According to both notions there was no alternative than for human beings to accept their fate. At best one could attempt to make the best of circumstances.

Classical bourgeois sociology overcame this determinism. Its theory is constructed on a dialectic between people who make their societies and society which itself makes a mark on people in the process of their socialization. A human being in the narrowest sense, a being who is at the same time both perennial and social, originates from a representative of the human genre by the internalizing of social reality. The process in which human beings and society determine each other takes place in a dynamic system in which the laws that they make themselves are also nevertheless real.[1]

One of the founding fathers of this discipline immediately supplemented this first basis of the sociological perspective with a second scheme. The nature and development of the social system is governed by human reality. Human beings want to shape their lives, their circumstances and the order of society purposively, rationally and in accordance with inward and outward conditions.[2] Because that is the case, an understanding of the order and the phenomena of society and culture can be read off the purposes and rationality of those who have created the social world.

However, in a third scheme in the framework, the role of rationality and the causality that can be inferred from it is toned down. Even the best purposes can have unexpected consequences, even more when it comes to a multiplicity of individual rationalities and aims. The 'unforeseeable consequences' are corrections of individual reality. So they too must be included in the reckoning.[3] They are in no way merely chance phenomena, but follow their own laws. If that is the case, there is also a possibility of discovering their logic.

The more complex the society, the more difficult it becomes to accept the inner coherence of the social system. Development brings a loss of transparency, and society and culture become more implausible. Social change accelerates. Perhaps in our time it has even taken a qualitative leap forward. There is much to indicate that the social world of the younger generation in highly-developed countries is no longer the same as that of the older generation. The consequences for less developed countries are obvious. Findings on the course converge. I shall outline them here.

From a sociological perspective, the modern socio-cultural development is called modernization. Its roots were formerly identified in the rise of bourgeois society, in industrialization and the Enlightenment. Today it is pointed out that this development became possible with Christianity, with the separation of the sacred and the profane. This then came to affect the social structure in the Investiture Dispute, in the separation of Pope and Emperor.

However far back the roots may go, solid experience of a new world came with the replacement of a country way of living by an urban, civic way of living. Not only the framework of life but also its nature, structure and constitution changed. The main dimensions of the change can be summed up relatively simply. Alongside direct contacts, the number of indirect contacts increased. The sphere of interpersonal relations was limited by the increase of formal, impersonal relations. The clear simplicity of the social world was replaced by a pluriform, complex totality of countless sub-systems of which even the parts were difficult to understand. The experience of a timeless, immutable and stable social milieu was disturbed by change, by the feeling that everything was short-term and provisional. The usefulness of yesterday's experiences and traditions gathered in history became questionable in the face of the discontinuities of social ties and the overall development and in the contingencies of the future. The social environment changed from a community to a society.[4]

The key concept in the change that I have described is social differentiation. An ever-increasing number of autonomous sub-systems (like politics, business, technology, science, the entertainment industry, communication, etc.) grew out of what was once a unitary social system with a hierarchical order. These have no common denominator, not even a generally recognized overarching authority to regulate them. Their relationship to one another and their totality as a social system is merely determined by mutual demarcation, rivalry and struggle, always with only provisional results which can only be relatively binding.

A community consists of natural persons, regardless of its internal rule and structures. An important property of modernity is the existence of persons in law and other corporate agents as elements in social life. In this field, the individual not only has to withstand other, possibly stronger, individuals, but is also confronted with institutions which have their own laws and their own cost-benefit calculations, follow their own morality and usually are far more powerful than individuals can ever be.[5]

There are advantages to a competitive situation. It can institutionalize a motivation which encourages achievement and the selection of the best. But it also has costs and disadvantages. Here are three of them. As complexity increases, the preservation of the capacity of the system to function presupposes an even greater increase in communication. The complexity produces uncertainties and risks which there is no ready-made process of dealing with and which cannot be derived from the system either. And finally, individuals are burdened with producing an order which suits them personally and a harmonious world of experience out of that differentiated world which intrinsically consists of parts with different structures, which are not tuned to one another.

Communication society?

There is hardly any other sphere in modern society which has expanded so markedly as that of public relations and the media. There may be no common denominator between the various areas of society, but at least they want to be informed about one another. The market and competition require information. People who have to know their way around a great variety of contexts also need information: quick, relevant, reliable and comprehensive. Change, new situations, the obsolescence of knowledge keep alive the need for ever new information. Up-to-dateness and the capacity to deal with the media and gain new information have become important criteria for advancement and success – in addition to the acquisition of a solid basic knowledge.

Perhaps it is possible to argue from the capacity for communication and the practice of communication to a unitary principle of order in the social world.[6] Perhaps without this argument we should regard communication as a means of 'interpenetration' and 'differentiation' in which the content of a system is turned into a system.[7] Perhaps it is even enough to stress the need for social exchange and information on the one hand and the means of communication on the other.[8] Be this as it may, the term 'communication society' seems to cover a central dimension of our social existence.[9] The significance of communication is not diminished by its becoming less a living relationship between two or more human partners, but more an independent system for the exchange of information with a richly equipped technical and economic arsenal.

Risk society?

A great many sociologists think that by their general differentiation, the systems of modern societies have lost all possibility of any higher authority as a point of reference of centre for integration. Here a trap has opened up. Competition leads to experiments, to new initiatives, to a risk society. But the multiplicity and diversity of subject-areas by no means excludes the possibility of generally accessible recipes and a generally valid way of dealing with accidents.

The problem of ordinary citizens begins with the impossibility of seeing through their environment. They do not know how trustworthy their bank is, how safe their aircraft is, what side-effects the fertilizer they use on their vegetables may have. Without the necessary specialist knowledge and relevant information, they hardly have any alternative than to trust that 'it will all work out!'[10] At most they can deny the dangers or relieve themselves of their responsibility by identifying scapegoats.[11]

A new feature of the situation is that citizens often have to put their trust in anonymous social agents. These refer to their experts and to safety which has been proved in practice, but in many respects they remain unknown, uncontrollable and vague. Modernity produces inconsistencies which present themselves to individuals as risks. Any progress produce new risks. Thus these are not accidental but structural properties. We are a society which puts itself in danger.

Beck calls our present society a 'risk society', because we have the technical possibility to destroy the world. The scale of doing this is a broad one, from pollution of the environment and the squandering of vital resources through the extermination of species of plants and animals to nuclear catastrophes. (Beck's study had just been written when the Chernobyl disaster took place.) Perhaps an even more important fact stands in the background. Modern society has uncoupled individual possibilities from public responsibilities. There are no powerful social mechanisms to confront the endangering of society and the future. The modern European and American world has created a new situation in two spheres. Individualization has made people independent of their social context and in part even immunized them. The same development has been completed in the change of values. Individual energies are no longer directed towards dominating nature or improving the political order, but towards the fostering of inwardness. These two steps call for further attention.

Individualization

Individualization has a long history[12] and many meanings. Some years ago, Riesman's sociological bestseller set people in the crowd (the characters directed from the outside) over against people guided by principles (those directed from within) and located individualism more in the second type than in the first.[13] Over the last two or three decades diagnoses have been mounting up which in fact note a decline in the significance of generally binding principles. However, the development does not seem to go in the direction of greater socialization and mutual adaptation. The individualism which can be identified in our times has different characteristics and elements. Three of its elements call for special attention: a situation of universal choice, a change of relationship to the world, and a continuing perception of multiplicity.

It begins with the pressure to decide. Whether it is a question of consumption, profession or human relations, there are many alternatives to choose from, and no prior social or other decisions are made which alter this fact. The 'surplus society' not only has more than enough commodities but also countless other possibilities. If a particular choice is expected in one milieu, then there are other milieus with other expectations. Social pressure in one case is countered with pressure in another direction in other contexts, in which one is equally involved. The decision about the direction in which to turn is left to the individual.

It is left to the individual to determine his or her own biography. And people often react to the uncertainty latent in freedom with a change of direction. They follow the fashion, change their job, their home, their acquaintances. Once the decision has been made, it remains related to the situation and also contingent in the given context. It can be revised or corrected at any time. The totality of the alternatives available is almost never known, nor is it possible to see all their details. So the choice is made largely by trial and error, which involves a long series of experiments. Even when there is relative success, the possibility cannot be ruled out that another decision could have led to better results. So the temptation to engage in new experiments remains, even in an unchanged situation. The slightest change in overall conditions leads to a re-examination of earlier options.

As though on shaky ground, modern men and women must be constantly prepared to change their position. For that they need a particular attitude and constant effort. Their view of the world inexorably changes. This view seems increasingly unstable, provisional, relative. Individual parts of the world may be autonomous and able to play off their autonomy against the individual. But the totality of the world does not have or communicate any structure or body of meaning which impose themselves on the individual. The relationship between human beings and the world is not ordered in terms of the world. Human beings must themselves make the order that they need; it does not come from the world. They themselves are the only stable point at their disposal. They are compelled to put themselves at the middle of the world and take the order that they conceive as their starting point. Earlier reflection on the ordering of the world is increasingly being suppressed by a relationship in which the world is draped over the individual. The notion of a stable world and the individual who is delivered over to it is being overtaken by the picture of an uncertain world in which at best the self offers some security.

The reversal of the relationship between the world and the person changes relative meanings. The self mutates from the cocoon of the cosmos to the God of itself and the world which it orders. Self-adoration is no longer in the way.[14] However, this self is not an abstract entity. It is embodied in a concrete way. In a world centred on itself a person's own body is very near the centre. The perception and the evaluation of the body and the attention that one pays to it changes.[15] The phenomena of the culture of the body and the beauty industry speak an eloquent language. But on the other hand, if the individual becomes the

Archimedean point of the world and its ultimate criteria, it is more than ever in need of explanation. The question of one's self is raised in countless variants. The quest for experience of the self and inwardness becomes the religious and profane programme, the fashion, the business.

The motif of individualism in the sense mentioned above is in no way a matter of egotism, but the need to bring order to a world which has lost it. However, the self-glorification of the power of the individual to bring order has its consequences. The new way of defining relationships calls for working on oneself, and so clearly touches on the domain of religion.[16] But it does not call for a change in the environment, or an active participation in public concerns. Individualism brings public life and social responsibility to a standstill.[17]

The experience of the plurality of the world and the contingency of one's own decision gnaws at the plausibility of existing general rules and norms. These divert into one's own hands and are also no longer expected of others. There are two opposed answers to this new human condition. A minority attempts to cling to the remains of former certainties, and flees into fundamentalism. Empirical research convincingly demonstrates that the great majority of people are increasingly content with the almost infinite variety of personal options and accept that other people are different.[18] The development extends from tolerance, through acceptance, to the permissive society, the members of which think anything acceptable which is not at their expense. The same attitude can also be read differently. Change opens up an understanding for the most different presuppositions and aims, and encourages empathy, the ability to put oneself in the position of others.

The thesis of individualization describes the consequences of the continuously increasing differentiation and the growing complexity of the social system. Its logic presupposes a constant socio-cultural development. By contrast, one school of research into the change of values presents international comparative data which locate a historical break on the chronological axis. These facts and the theory that goes with them complete the picture so far.

Values and a change in values

European and American research has countless findings which show that the values, attitudes and world-view of the 'post-war generation' are qualitatively different from those of older generations.[19] The difference can only partly be explained by the usual changes between age-groups or generations. The sociology of values regards the fundamental change in the economic conditions of life as the main cause of this change. A fundamental shift has been taking place in economic living conditions in the middle of the twentieth century. There is much talk of the transition from a society of lack to a society of surplus (or even a throwaway society). The older generation had to concentrate on the material safeguarding of existence and the overcoming of economic uncertainties. Children who have been born into a prosperous society take these things for granted and can therefore set themselves other, non-material goals. The norm is provided not so much by current living conditions as by the effect of socialization. The generation which was once prepared for want perpetually maintains an attitude orientated on gain and a quest for guarantees.

Membership of the pre-war or post-war generation has two consequences. The first is a deep difference in world-view and order of values, in other words a polarization of society by age. Secondly, this interpretation carries with it the prognosis that the development is in the direction of the prosperous society and the corresponding order of values. The future belongs to it.

For the sake of simplicity (and for public effect), one order of values has been called 'materialistic' and the other 'post-materialistic'.[20] 'Materialistic' has been used as a collective term for prosperity and security. The indicators used have ranged from the fight against inflation, the maintaining of economic stability, the encouragement of economic growth, law and order, and strong defence capabilities to the fight against criminality. 'Post-materialistic' has designated a democratic outlook, a concern for the environment and a preference for the ideal. The values and preferences mentioned extend from the protection of freedom of speech, through political participation, a say in the affairs of home locality and work-place, the beautification of villages and town, to the point of the development of a more human world and a society in which ideas are more important than money.[21]

The concept of the 'experience society' is to be understood as a combination of the thesis of individualism and the thesis of a change in values.[22] In addition it is open to argument how far an empirical study on a relatively narrow basis, which provides the starting point, can be generalized. In any case this work is a seamless continuation of the two theses mentioned. Differences in style which arise from the break in generations and the differences in level of education are documented. The new emphasis is provided with the search for experience.

The thesis of individualism had left open the question whether the individual is turning inwards completely or developing a new form of being sociable, possibly one which accepts the freedom and identity of other people more than was the case in previous cultures. There was similarly a positive evaluation in the notion of post-materialism. There a development was indicated, from the values of the safeguarding of existence to those of self-development. The concept of the experience society speaks openly of 'self-realization anchored in the "I"'. This is hardly distinguishable from naked egotism. (However, one inconsistency in the findings consists in the large circles of friends found in parts of this type and the tendency towards alternative movements.) The dominant tension in the experience society is that between needs and the satisfying of experiences. Furthermore, in order not to have to put all human striving by satisfying it, the stimulation of provocative experience has a function of its own.

The experience society may merely represent one of the possible alternatives of development. But the ways to that and many signs of its existence are manifest. Its significance for the functioning of society and the realization of being a Christian may be similarly clear.[23]

Outside the society of surplus and experience

The levelling out of former class distinctions and the achievement of a general state of prosperity are important developments in the highly-developed Western world. The everyday experience of these facts often leads to a strange narrowing of perception. Citizens of the post-industrial society and sociologists who report on it quite often start tacitly or even explicitly by assuming that their milieu can be identified with the world generally, or at least that the whole world is tending towards where they already are. There is insufficient basis for this view. Perhaps the society of surplus and experience cannot be limited geographically. But it is the milieu of less than a quarter of humankind. And the majority are not at an unattainable distance. Some are on our doorsteps, in the growing group of pensioners, unemployed, homeless, handicapped, etc. The assumption of the universal validity of the forms of life sketched out is certainly false, and the development in that direction is at least questionable.

However, the narrowing of perception is not a chance disease nor an expression of individual sinfulness, but a flight from the impotence caused by the complexity of the world, a structural consequence of individualism and the experience society. The world order that has been put together can be kept free of conflict if one leaves conflicts out of account or represses them. Modern inwardness easily leads to a shift from social responsibility and solidarity. Above all those countries and classes who have no chance of participating in the society of prosperity and experience have to suffer the consequences.

Translated by John Bowden

Notes

1. Peter Berger and Thomas Luckmann, *The Social Construction of Reality*, Garden City, NY 1966.
2. Wolfgang Schluchter, *Rationalität der Weltbeherrschung. Studien zu Max Weber*, Frankfurt am Main 1980.
3. Robert K. Merton, 'The Unanticipated Consequences of Purposive Social Action', *American Sociological Review* 1, 1936, 894–904.
4. Ferdinand Tönnies, *Gemeinschaft und Gesellschaft* (1887), Darmstadt 1972.
5. James S. Coleman, *The Asymmetric Society*, Syracuse, NY 1982.
6. Jürgen Habermas, *Theory of Communicative Action* (3 vols), Oxford 1985–9; *Philosophical Discourse of Modernity*, Oxford 1988.
7. Niklas Luhmann, *Soziale Systeme*, Frankfurt am Main 1984.
8. Colin Cherry, *On Human Communication*, New York 1956.
9. Richard Münch, *Dialektik der Kommunikationsgesellschaft*, Frankfurt am Main 1991.
10. Anthony Giddens, *The Consequences of Modernity*, Oxford 1990.
11. Ulrich Beck, *Risikogesellschaft. Auf dem Weg in eine andere Moderne*, Frankfurt am Main 1986; Zygmunt Bauman, *Modernity and Ambivalence*, Oxford 1991.
12. Louis Dumont, *Essais sur l'individualisme. Une perspective anthropologique sur l'idéologie moderne*, Paris 1983.
13. David Riesman, Reuel Denny and Nathan Glazer, *The Lonely Crowd. A Study of the Changing American Character*, New Haven 1950.
14. Christopher Lasch, *The Culture of Narcissism*, New York 1978.
15. Mike Featherstone, Mike Hepworth and Bryan G. Turner (eds), *The Body. Social Process and Cultural Theory*, London and New Delhi 1995.
16. Karl Gabriel (ed.), *Religiöse Individualisierung oder Säkularisierung. Biographie und Gruppe als Bezugspunkte moderner Religiosität*, Gütersloh 1996.
17. Richard Sennett, *The Fall of Public Man*, New York 1974.
18. Peter Ester, Loek Halman and Ruud de Moor (eds), *The Individualizing Society. Change in Europe and Northern America*, Tilburg 1994; Torlief Pettersson and Ole Riis (eds), *Scandinavian Values. Religion and Morality in the Nordic Countries*, Uppsala 1994.
19. Ronald Inglehart, *Modernization and Postmodernization. Cultural, Economic and Political Change in 43 Societies*, Princeton 1997; Clark Wade Roof, Jackson W. Carrol and David A. Roozen (eds), *The Post-War Generation and Established Religion. Cross-Cultural Perspectives*, Boulder, Colorado 1995.

20. Helmut Klages, Hans-Jürgen Hippler and Willi Herbert, *Werte und Wandel*, Frankfurt and New York 1992; Ronald Inglehart, *Cultural Change*, Princeton 1989.

21. Paul R. Abrahamson and Ronald Inglehart, *Value Change in Global Perspective*, Ann Arbor, Michigan 1989.

22. Gerhard Schulze, *Die Erlebnisgesellschaft. Kultursoziologie der Gegenwart*, Frankfurt and New York 1992.

23. Hermann Kochanek, 'Die Erlebnisgesellschaft – eine postmoderne Herausforderung für Seelsorge und Pastoral', in id. (ed.), *Religion und Glaube in der Postmoderne*, Nettetal 1995, 151–220.

III · Theological Interpretations

The Dangerous Memory of Jesus Christ in a Post-Traditional Society

Alberto Moreira

Memory in post-traditional society

There is a scene in Ridley Scott's film 'Blade Runner' that provides a paradigmatic illustration of the subject of this article. The secretary of the great entrepreneur who creates androids is faced with the suspicion that she too is an android, a hybrid being built specifically to suit the needs of her boss. She defends her human identity by appealing to her childhood memories, something that androids obviously do not have, since they were made to last just four years. The detective hunting androids then shows her that these memories were implanted by her boss and creator. They are really the childhood memories of another person (her boss' daughter), remembrances of a life she never lived, put into her like an alien soul. The 'identity' that has always provided her with an 'identification' was not hers but that of a stranger, placed in her from within by her creator and 'father'. Her memories, though pleasant and sweet, had no past, were not *her* history. Borrowed memory lent her an inauthentic existence. As a result, her own existence was nothing more than an expression of the interests and convenience of an industrialist belonging to the chemical-biological and military complex.

While in traditional societies the dead were always present in the lives of the living, and so also oppressed them, since tradition imposes itself through its rituals, its inviolable norms and its coercive apparatus, post-traditional societies, on the other hand, bury the memory of their dead under a mountain of consumer goods, a vast mass of unnecessary information and a frenetic rhythm of life whose fragments of experience shift and pile up like those of a kaleidoscope. Capitalism, by generating an immediatist culture with its notion of homogeneous and empty time,[1] has buried its dead for a second time by producing the (even more potent) myth of an eternal present, or of the return of the ever-the-same disguised as technological progress. It is an eternal present that has to be lived under the sign of instant satisfaction, of immediate return on investment and of compulsory amusement.

Memory, time and history in critical thought

Walter Benjamin made an acute and dramatic examination of the question of time and history in the Fascist era of capitalism, unmasking belief in the inevitability of technological progress – based on the victims it produced – as a second-degree myth. Both the myth of progress and the archaic myth made the unfolding of history appear to people's minds as something alienated from human activity. For Benjamin, capitalist progress was like a storm piling ruins on ruins.[2] Over against homogenous time bereft of quality, there still exists a *present time*: the messianic time, in which the victims, starting from an acute hermeneutical sensitivity to danger[3] and a perception of *time as term*, break the stranglehold of empty and homogenous time through remembering the disasters and injustices they have experienced in the past. For Benjamin, whose thought was influenced by Jewish theology, only theological thinking enables one to view the past as not-finished, not definitively past, and is capable of giving weight to both present needs for justice and the rights and dreams of the victims of history.[4] This understanding requires a critical stance, imagination and resultant action. It also produced Benjamin's perception, tragically confirmed by his death, that the time remaining makes this (re)action ever more pressing.

Taking up Benjamin's perceptions, Theodor Adorno saw the destruction of relationship with the dead as a symptom of 'the sickness of experience today'.[5] For him, weakening or impoverishment of experience comes about when the experiences and contents evoked no longer arise freely and involuntarily in memory but are culturally and socially induced and pre-programmed. So the reification and alienation of understanding come, according to Adorno, from socially engendered inability to experience freely and spontaneously. The exchange model of buying and selling in the market tends to eliminate or to co-opt everything that does not fit in with its calculations of cost-benefit time: time, memory, tradition, 'What is not proven here and now to be socially useful to the market has no value and is forgotten' (GS 10, 311). Even memory of one's own suffering, including that caused by society, has to be set aside so as not to hinder the 'onward march' and not to upset the identification of the individual with the system.

Even so, since the source of suffering never dries up, society needs to create and develop an 'industry of oblivion', which masks and sustains false reconciliation between individuals and the system that oppresses them. The very society that produces suffering and exclusion develops mechanisms to make people forget them: 'It is of the essence of domination to prevent recognition of the suffering it produces of itself.'[6] This would basically constitute the function of the industry of culture: to entertain in order to make people forget. Adorno saw that it replaced people's experience of their own sufferings with cultural products and with the reduction of auto-perception to stereotypical concepts belonging to market culture. For him, it is only the resistance provided by pain and suffering to discursive cognition that allows the logic of instrumental reasoning to be breached. Through these cracks grows understanding of the non-identity between individual and system, between the oppressive generalization and oppressed individuals (who at the same time help to keep the system that oppresses them in being). Suffering actualizes the corporeal moment of cognition, which prevents its identification with discursive thought. Suffering sets a limit to thinking itself, which thought can recognize as its own, and so, in suffering, the subject sees how little discursive (systematic) logic affects his own thought reality. This produces the possibility of an 'estrangement' with respect to this oppressive quasi-totality. 'Suffering as the flesh-and-blood moment of experience imposes a limit on the tendency to conform to what exists.' In this confirmation with the memory of their own pain and that of others, people work out and affirm their own identity, however fragile: an identity of refusal of the abstract reasoning of meta-discourses and of resistance to the causes of suffering.

Memory therefore appears as an essential ingredient of authentic and non-domesticated experience, just as reified understanding is characterized precisely by forgetting. The de-temporizing of experience and its weakening go hand in hand. Adorno holds that 'any reification is a forgetting' and 'critique means precisely the same as memory, in other words mobilizing in phenomena that which turned them out and makes them what they are, and through this realizing the possibilities that they could have turned out Different and therefore can be Different'.[7] It is not a question of preserving tradition at all costs: 'It is not in order to conserve the past, but in order to realize a past hope that we engage in action' (*DA*, GS 3, 15). In our relation with the past, there is a 'productive memory', which should 'on the one hand relive its isolation, its character of being-past, without, on the other, trying to produce a false proximity, which would eliminate its difference and its non-identity'. It is just through its estrangement and exaggeration that this memory can become productive as it critiques, discomforts, unmasks or scandalizes the present. The memory of one's own suffering and that of others, of those conquered, wronged and maltreated by history, possesses an *authority* that speaks for itself. This authority of pain is an imperative that ordains its overcoming, a motive force that nourishes practice and spirituality to make the cause of suffering cease. In Adorno's terms, this known imperative requires people so to 'dispose their thought and action that Auschwitz is not repeated, that nothing similar happens' again (*Negative Dialektik*, GS 6, 358). It is above all a matter of preventing barbarism from becoming established and to work to this end with the sense of clarity and urgency that the situation demands. The specific attitude in which resistance is expressed is that of refusal to collaborate with what the system imposes. Adorno also sees possibilities for liberating the energies of individuals to face up to control by systems in history in *mimesis* (the archaic spontaneity of the corporeal and the somatic), in *aesthetic experience*, and even in a *non-idealist metaphysic*, rooted in material existence.

The concept of dangerous memory in the work of J.-B. Metz

In dialogue with the thinkers of the Frankfurt School and others, J.-B. Metz in his works developed the theological concept of the *subversive or dangerous memory of Jesus Christ*, which became a key concept in political theology.[8] At least since 1968 Metz has been working on and deepening the significance of the *memoria passionis, mortis et resurrectionis Jesu Christi* in order to construct a political theology.[9] For him, memory is one of the basic categories, together with solidarity and narrativity, of a fundamental non-idealist theology, concerned to impinge on people's lives and guide their actions. In this sense, memory is a category shot through with *praxis* and, like the other two, is bound up with theological concepts that both describe it and ground it: 'practice of following', 'suffering', 'witness'. For Metz, *memoria passionis et resurrectionis* fundamentally indicates the anamnetic identity of Christianity. The community of men and women followers of Christ, in the beginning and the present, is formed on the basis of calling to mind the life, passion and death of Jesus and of the experience of salvation that burst forth in the resurrection of the Crucified, as promise of final and eschatological liberation for all, especially for the crucified of history. It is in the power of and trust in the very Spirit of Jesus, which inspires and sustains the community of his followers, that Christian women and men take on the commitment to keep this memory of suffering alive in the today of history and bind themselves to active solidarity with all women and men affected by any form of injustice, pain, oppression and wrongdoing. The memory of Christ is the way in which Christians show, in narrative and practical form, their eschatological hope in history and in society.[10] Believing in the Christian sense means adopting a posture in which people recall the promises made by God and the hopes experienced because of them, uniting themselves to these memories and moulding their lives to them (GGG 176). So it is clear that these memories are not merely ritual, resigned or traditionalist, or the sanitized survival of a dead man. This is a *dangerous memory*, assaulting the present with its unfulfilled demands, with its repressed conflicts and its open wounds (GGG 161ff.). This *subversive memory* takes on the sufferings and dreams of those who have fallen on the way, and yet in both society and the church it shows itself as much as *retrospective solidarity* as it does as *eschatological hope* that such promises will be fulfilled in the future.

As E. Zenger has shown, the culture of Israel itself is 'an anamnetic culture', entirely governed by the dynamic of 'what we cannot forget – for the sake of our lives'. This is an archaic principle of Jewish life: 'Look and remember!' (*samor wezakor*). 'From its remembrances of God and within them, Israel was capable of surviving all (including Christian-inspired) attempts to destroy it.'[11] Therefore, the dangerous calling to mind of Christ, around which Christians come together and which has formed their identity in the 'confrontations and dangers of history',[12] even though it has so often been betrayed and forgotten, is a category of liberation and of encounter-preservation for Christians. The church is formed precisely when people take up this legacy and become the subjects of their own stories, of their memories, symbols and practices of faith. This anamnetic identity protects Christians against the conquering idols of society, strengthens their resistance to deceits and any temptation to triumphalism, and serves as a basic hermeneutic criterion for any use of practical-critical reason. The memory of suffering should remain as a thorn in the flesh of reasoning, including theological reasoning, to save it from its cynicism.

The remembrance of Jesus is dangerous and subversive because it attacks the today of history and calls it into question; it prevents us from passing over barbarities committed, injustices unremedied, sufferings unconsoled and ongoing, re-created each day through the systems of oppression and control of individuals. The memory of Jesus is dangerous because it recalls his life and his practice of freedom in our postmodern climate of apparent freedom, in which the very desire for freedom is in fact manipulated. It is in this historical situation that individuals are struggling to decide their lives and their future; it is in the present that the fate of those who suffer to make themselves heard, to be respected in their rights, is played out: tomorrow may be too late. Where are their allies? On whom can they count? Danger, actual threats, provide an apocalyptic backdrop to action, to the active and effective practice of solidarity (GGG 54, 69–74, 204–11). In effect, this eschatological reserve challenges both idealistic discourses and the conquerors' version of history, both social Darwinism and the compression of history into the consumerist present, its supposed end according to ideologues of the Fukuyama school. So it emerges clearly that the dangerous remembrance of Christ in the world is both a hermeneutic and ecclesiological category and a political category of resistance and struggle.

This dangerous and liberating memory of the liberty of Christ, on which our freedom is based, can only be *narrated*, recounted henceforth in the personal experience of faith and practice. This makes narrative another concept that is inseparable from memory (GGG 63f., 145f., 173f., 181–94). To take up an expression of Carlos Mesters' referring to base church communities, it is a 'defenceless flower', a 'treasure we carry in earthenware vessels', which needs to be kept alive in the telling and protected with arguments in the modern world. Finally, the concept of *dangerous memory of Christ* also represents a privileged *locus theologicus* for reflection on the question of God in the present situation. Recalling and re-proposing speech of and on God in a postmodern situation where we are tired and forgetful of God, but which paradoxically cultivates new myths and new gods, means re-presenting to the consciousness of a forgotten humanity the suffering of forgotten human beings, from whom society protects itself and whose remembrance it tries to forget. Furthermore, 'this theodicy is a question that refers back to (the very) God – God himself will be sure, "in his Day", to justify himself through the abysmal history of the suffering of the world, of "his world" '.[13]

Such a theological sensibility, deriving from negative theology, is more than just a method: it forms an interpretative horizon, which has constituted the theologies worked out since Vatican II (political, liberation, black, feminist, Indian and other). These unite the reality of human suffering to theology about God and the discourse on God to the memory of those who suffer injustice and discrimination. Liberation theology, for example, is fundamentally shot through with anamnetic motifs: the delivery from slavery in Egypt, the question of the poor as a question of God, the spirituality of conflict, the principle of mercy, the memory of the martyrs.[14]

How does this constellation of theological criteria and hermeneutic categories incide on life and social and ecclesial praxis in post-traditional societies? It is without any doubt as absence and negation that the concept of memory critiques reality, questions the church, and should work productively on Christian practice. In the light of this we have to say that it is no longer possible, without being cynical, to defend any religious experience or theological thought that – turning its back on the history of human suffering – cultivates encounter and contact with God. Yet this is precisely what the 'light', holistic and aseptic spirituality of many types of postmodern religious and pseudo-philosophical movements does, inside and outside the churches. These engage in mass forgetfulness of history, including the history of domination within Christianity itself, and make light of the negative aspects of market culture. The pragmatic and immediatist rationale of instantaneous gratification has penetrated Christianity and world religions. The so-called theology of prosperity, produced in the USA and much in vogue in poor countries, demands here and now a worldly, intra-historical eschatology: the immediate fulfilment of all promises of well-being and prosperity as a sign of God's blessing. The spectactularization of faith requires great media-type events, celebrities, religious shows laden with much emotion and little discernment, which promise instant union with God. At the same time, the quest for 'therapies' of all kinds seems to show the existence of a generalized perception that the human condition is one of suffering. So the system profits twice from individuals: it produces their fatigue, loneliness and despair, and then sells them the 'spiritual healing' in the shape of telephone conversations with the horde of magicians, astrologers and quacks of all sorts who infest their television screens.

One characteristic of the postmodern cosmovision is freedom of choice for individuals to set up their own meaning-systems, or their own religious universe. So new niches of belonging are created. Such a process provides a high point of emancipation of individuals from institutionalized religious mediations and of affirmation of their creative capacity. On the other hand, this new freedom is confined to freedom of consumer choice; people are able to choose only from a stock of pre-fabricated meaning-systems, 'made-to-measure' for their needs. It is against this changed horizon that the church should see itself as 'public and ongoing witness to a dangerous memory among the systems of our emancipatory society' (Metz, GGG 78). Unfortunately, Roman-curial authoritarian formalism has immobilized the greater number of Catholic Christians to the point where they still look to and totally depend on their priest, bishop and pope.[15] Will we become capable of forming groups and communities through affinity of choice and not just through cultural imitation – anamnetic communities and not just sacramentalized ones?

The dangerous memory of the martyrs and the resistance of the victims

The ecumenical experience of a demanding faith, which prolongs the dangerous memory of Jesus Christ in the present, can still be found in many communities, groups and movements throughout the world. It needs to be said that the victims themselves are resisting, not accepting their neglect by society and the church and not waiting passively for the end. To make their clamour heard they and their allies continue taking to the streets, beating on empty doors, going on hunger strikes, occupying government buildings, ransacking supermarkets, taking to the sea in small boats, trying to cross barriers and frontiers, organizing marches great and small, occupying land, coming together in base communities, forming human chains, defending life and democracy where they are threatened.

In some churches and communities this subversive memory of Jesus is made immediately present through celebrating the memory of their martyrs. As in other parts of the world, in some churches in Latin America we celebrate the eucharist around remembrance of our heroines and heroes. We set out their photographs and portraits; we read their letters and writings with feeling; we walk to the places where they were assassinated; we tell one another the stories of their lives; we call to mind their courage; we console ourselves with their same faith and commitment. Josimo, Ellacuría, Santo Dias, Marçal, Margarida, Adélia, Oscar Romero, Penido Burnier, Expedito and so many others – the people for whom they lived and died regard them as saints. They are saints who worked impressive miracles of justice, love and conversion, but have not the slightest chance of being beatified by the curial church of John Paul II. Many were not killed but underwent great sufferings, and we consider them equally worthy witnesses to the faith. Several of them also suffered because of the church, suffering that it, unfortunately, still doles out to many of its 'daughters' and 'sons'. These Christians, like so many unknown good Samaritans throughout the world, will not fade away: 'In the presence of a crucified people their bowels were stirred and they were moved to mercy.'[16]

For all their sakes, may I express the hope that the dangerous and subversive memory of Jesus Christ, fragile and mysterious as it is, may remain alive in the world. Beneath the ashes the fire has not gone out.

Translated by Paul Burns

Notes

1. Cf. W. Benjamin, 'Thesen über den Begriff der Geschichte', in R. Tiedemann and H. Schweppenhäuser (eds), *GS*, Vol. 1, Frankfurt 1974, 700ff.
2. O. John, ' "Und dieser Feind hat zu siegen nicht aufgehört". Die Bedeutung W. Benjamins für eine Theologie nach Auschwitz', Münster dissertation 1982, 430. D. Wilhelm, *Eingedenken – eine gefährdete feministiche Kategorie*, Münster thesis 1989, 23, 27.
3. O. John, 'Im Augenblick der Gefahr', cited by Wilhelm, *Eingedenken* (n. 2), 13.
4. Wilhelm, *Eingedenken* (n. 2), 62.
5. *Dialektik der Aufklärung (DA)*, Vol. 3 of *Gesammelte Schriften (GS)*, Frankfurt 1981, 243. For the discussion of Adorno I am indebted to J. A. Zamora, *Krise-Kritik-Erinnerung. Ein politisch – theologischer Versuch über das Denken Adornos im Horizon – der Krise der Moderne*, Münster 1995.
6. T. Adorno, *Minima Moralia*, London 1979.
7. *Einleitung in die Soziologie*, 250.
8. Cf. J.-B. Metz, 'Erinnerung', in H. Krings, H. M. Baumgartner and C. Wild (eds), *Handbuch philosophischer Grundbegriffe*, Vol. 2, Munich 1973, 386–96; *Glaube in Geschichte und Gesellschaft*, Mainz [4]1984 (GGG).
9. For a detailed analysis of the concept see X. Bischof, 'Der Begriff "Erinnerung" in der politischen Theologie von J.-B. Metz', Theological Faculty of Lucerne 1980.
10. GGG 161; Bischof, ' "Erinnerung" ', 3.
11. 'Von der rettenden Kraft der jüdischen Gotteserinnerung', in T. Peters, T. Pröpper and H. Steinkamp (eds), *Erinnern und Erkennen. Denkanstösse aus der Theologie von J.-B. Metz*, Düsseldorf 1993, 16.
12. GGG 63.
13. T. Pröpper, 'Fragende und Gefragte zugleich. Notizen zur Theodizee', in Peters *et al.*, *Erinnern und Erkennen* (n. 11), 62.
14. I. Ellacuría and J. Sobrino (eds), *Mysterium Liberationis. Fundamental Concepts of Liberation Theology*, Maryknoll 1993.

15. Cf. J. Comblin, 'O Cristianismo no limiar do Terceiro Milênio', in C. Caliman (ed.), *A sedução do sagrado*, Petrópolis 1998.

16. J. Sobrino, *O Principio Misericórdia*, Petrópolis 1994, 254.

Instant Gratification and Liberation

Ferdinand Dagmang

The earliest body of liberation theology and literature had a propensity to belabour the point of oppression of the Latin American poor. The mediation of the social sciences for theological analysis was considered necessary. Even in the ensuing years, as a later generation of liberation theologians struggled to articulate a more theoretical foundation for liberation theology, the socio-political agenda still determined the direction of their theories/propositions.[1] In recent years, as other forms of oppression (gender, racial, ecological) captured attention, many liberationists took time to apply other tools of analysis in the study of various social issues. What is noteworthy in these latter efforts is the eventual enrichment of the understanding of the meaning and cause of liberation as a more nuanced meaning of oppression became available.

Instant gratification is one issue which should stimulate inquiry and enrich our understanding of and commitment to liberating action. An object (instant gratification) examined with the cause of liberation in mind must, however, clear the way for a mode of analysis which is thoroughly suspicious. This form of analysis proceeds with careful unearthing, hoping that in the process one could contribute to the cause of unmasking areas or conditions of life which are taken for granted as plainly natural (but once exposed, their operations are really shown to be inimical to the promotion of freedom or unfavourable to our desire to promote Christian solidarity). In other words, the concern for liberation cannot avoid a critical reflection of the meaning of any situation which could threaten human emancipation. A liberationist interpretation/grasp of the meaning of instant gratification must adopt a mode of analysis which faces up to the challenge of liberation.

Instant gratification and oppression

For many people, the offer of instant gratification is an offer of greater freedom from constraints to immediate satisfaction of needs and wants. Certainly people consider the limited and belated supply of goods and services as a form of burden. That is why we can say that many people are bearers of an orientation (the subject pole) towards instant gratification. On the other hand, one could also question the plethora of goods and services (the object pole) as imposing another form of burden. In other words, the existence of 'instant gratification' could also mean the presence of oppression.

We cannot assume that the offer of or orientation to instant gratification is thoroughly oppressive. What can be done, initially, is to bring out background or foreground information that could shed light on the fact of instant gratification. Hopefully, our findings could contribute to our commitment towards liberation even from things regarded as innocuous, as they are taken for granted as necessary.

Producers and their goods – the offer of instantly gratifying objects

In our world, goods are sold as 'gratifying objects' for consumers. Within contexts dominated by the global capitalistic market, what is gratifying or fulfilling is not solely for the consumers to determine but also for the producers or investors. People who produce their own goods for consumption have the freedom to determine what is gratifying or fulfilling for them. The question of what is gratifying for most consumers who merely buy what they need may only be answered by their cash supply and the market's inventory. Today, consumers need not worry about availability since the market is flooded with all kinds of goods. What they have to worry about, if they are aware of it, is the way the market is saturated with goods that do not necessarily benefit them. The most saleable items in the market need not have started as necessities. Most of them became profitable because of the astute handling of their producers or manufacturers. Think of how Coca-Cola or Chiclets started and eventually flourished.

In most less-urbanized or traditional societies (including the poorer and still developing societies) where we find persons or groups producing their own consumable goods, we also find the element of waiting-in-patience before actual consumption and gratification. The waiting-in-patience component of production–consumption was somehow part of the whole story of gratification, as families and clans (or people in closely-knit communities) worked patiently to produce their own goods. It was normal to wait patiently for the brewing of a very satisfying barrel of beer; for the ageing of a most exhilarating drink; for the careful knitting of clothing material for quality pullovers. In most cases, in instances of patient waiting, a certain form of 'postponement' of gratification is welcome. 'Postponement' in this case is quite an anachronism. To postpone gratification already implies individual capacity and the objective possibility of bringing about gratification. In many pre-modern cases, postponement is unavoidable, both subjectively and objectively. Many subjects are naturally waiting for the produce and the object of their desires. In today's market, objects are created even before subjects are aware of them. Objects of desire are already there even before subjects could desire them.

As more complex patterns of production, exchange and consumption of goods developed, the supply and availability of objects became overwhelming. As more 'alien' goods have been introduced into the market, many people who knew nothing of new products are no longer aware of the mediating waiting-in-patience factor for production and gratification. Hence, gratification can no longer account for waiting-in-patience, since it is now divorced from patient work-production.

As goods become more abundant, subjects are now bombarded by many stimulating objects of desire. Such overwhelming omnipresent 'alien' objects disturb focus and tend to overpower freedom of choice. They even induce in many a forgetfulness about what was once considered as fundamental kind of work: work to produce goods for one's needs and pleasures. Almost everybody now takes for granted the necessity of another kind of work: full-time work to earn money in order to acquire goods for the satisfaction of needs and wants. People have to work patiently for money in order to buy products ready-made or prepared by others who are not necessarily one's associates or acquaintances.[2] Consumption of products will now involve buying from markets controlled by people whose main end is not sharing but earning money. This is done mainly through the process of impersonal commercial transactions.

Goods and services produced and sold in the impersonal markets of capitalism are to be assumed to be potentially gratifying. The capitalist market's drive to manufacture and offer these goods and services are correlates of every consumer's desires and needs. Necessarily, the handlers of the market do not just produce goods and services; they work in view of every consumer's desire and potential need for products. They also see to it that consent among consumers will be manufactured through more and more sophisticated and efficient advertising. Thus, we find in the global market the development of a highly rationalized (strategized) systems of production/marketing which try to set acceptable levels and patterns of acquisition and consumption. This dynamic of production-acquisition-consumption is well-monitored, while incessantly pounding on consumers' longing for gratification.

One of the most successful ways of inducing desire and manufacturing consent is the promise of instant gratification. The market's offer of instant gratification may come in two ways: first, in the availability of products; second, in their functionality or effectiveness.

Gratification is already announced by producers and felt by consumers with the availability or even with the promise of availability of instantly consumable food, sex, sports, clothes, information and other things including religion. Individuals open to the suggestions of the media and other information outlets are captured by a deluge of choice data that stimulate attention, attract support, maintain patronage and disseminate favourable opinions about certain goods and services. Many products are already packaged and offered as gratifying even before they are tried and tested by the public. Their acceptability already rests on well-publicized approval ratings by public and consumer proxies such as the in-house scientific research team, state controls, consumer societies, media, etc. In other words, subjects who acquire such goods are not entirely free to exercise first-hand critical choice, since a whole bundle of determining factors is already let loose even before they see the products. What individuals may consume is no longer dictated by a choice of what to produce since they no longer produce what they consume. Others are frustrated at times because what they need to acquire or consume is no longer sold in the market, since producers ceased producing them for lack of a determined number of consumers.

Even if a product has been in the market for years and is already enjoying a seal of superior quality and a track record of public acceptability measured by sales and profits, its handlers cannot sit in passive contentment and allow popularity be in charge of the product's future. With the challenges posed by competitors, with the discoveries of new technologies and raw materials, with the consumers' ceaseless search for what satisfies or excites, etc., market handlers are in constant search for ways to maintain their hold on people as well as expand their turf. All factors considered, the question of consumer gratification is the most important, and as a result a whole culture of gratification-orientated marketing dominates our market-orientated society. Thus, products packaged with guarantees of satisfaction and consumer options like 'three-day testing' or 'return if not satisfied' are very common.

Today, things for sale are already here even before one is born. Products made by others for our consumption are already there, making many of us consumers of others' products. Certain patterns of production and acquisition/consumption have developed and function as moulds into which personalities are shaped. Everyone becomes accustomed to these patterns of our society driven by the complex mechanics of production and acquisition/consumption.

Some products or goods are offered to satisfy the basic needs of people, while others are meant to satisfy one's search for 'higher' things. The former are more aptly terms as 'gratifying', while the latter may be more appropriately called 'fulfilling'. Both goods, however, are now items for sale. The best detergent and the best counselling for self-fulfilment are available for those who can pay for them. Seen from the perspective of the world capitalistic market, sandwiches, health, leisure, education, security and divine blessing have something in common: a price tag.

Producers, in their constant search for saleable goods, pre-empt consumers' needs by introducing products which are a substitute for the real. In some overly congested and polluted cities, oxygen packs (fresh air) are already for sale. One's need for someone to nurture is even fed by the market's newly-developed toys (*tamagochi*).

Consumers, in their habit of searching for greater stimuli, help the producers manufacture goods with exciting features. In some cases, gratification and fulfilment become synonymous with excitement. Eventually, consumers (many people) develop the habit of judging other goods, including the more intangible ones (like intimacy, friendship and love), according to their capacity to excite. This is an instance where the values of the market could twist people's judgment at the expense of the more substantive human values dear to many cultures.

Subjects and their needs – the dis-orientation to instant gratification

In many poorer nations,[3] aside from the low-salary schemes perpetrated by majority of business firms, the lack of social security benefits and the perennial economic crises, the more fundamental forms of oppression come hand-in-hand with work. Today, the form of work one does as an employee is hardly devoid of attributes of alienation.

A lot of self-expression that forms part of work is estranged from the workers. What could give them gratification (the product itself, the enjoyment of the process of production, their fellowship with co-workers, and their ambitions fulfilled) are neither available to nor fully enjoyed by the workers. In many work set-ups, one's labour could hardly be at the same time one's vocation. Workers neither labour to produce what they consume nor participate in the whole process of production.

We know how a good number of people in many poorer countries are forced to take up roles they do not like, just to meet the demands of survival. These people usually do not find in those roles the fulfilment that they are longing for. The factories or the offices are not the usual places where people could experience genuine self-affirmation and fulfilment. People are not happy in monotonous and business-aligned jobs. In these places, most patterns of activities do not promote free expression of ambitions, legitimate aspirations or calling. They are even counter-productive, in the sense that they do not engender a more relaxed, free and thus joyful disposition – a basic disposition that could promote generosity and co-operation among workers. Take the case of a worker in a canning factory. If he is assigned to press sardines into cans before they are finally sealed, every second he will be pressing a can brought by the conveyor belt operating for seven to nine hours and moving 20,000 to 30,000 cans a day. This is his assignment for the whole day, for the whole week, for the whole year. A year of work yields 6 million monotonous strokes, and this is not at all enjoyable. It is punishing drudgery. In his post, the worker looks forward to very short breaks and to the end of the day, and so probably rushes home or to some other place. Workers are, of course, happier and relaxed in leisure activities. Not a few of them find happiness and fulfilment in the simple appreciation of wife, children or select friends.

Moreover, 'normal' interactions usually are not possible because in many places work is too specialized, strictly controlled, monotonous and usually not to one's own inclination. The factory setting, monotonous work in offices, dull and disheartening government service, many single-parent households or even a household where either the husband or the wife is habitually absent, are areas of life where self-satisfaction is very low in supply and where self-esteem could also be precarious. In these settings we find many subjects deprived of the essential forms of gratification. Eventually they form part of that whole reserved army of potential subjects seeking gratification – the same multitude whose appetite and capacity to pay become the consumer mass base of the market stock of producers and investors.

On the surface of things, the presence of goods and the need for them presents a symbiosis for the maintenance of a whole network of relationships natural to a market set-up. Classical economics may not question the existing division of labour, the taken-for-granted buy and sell format, the notion of private property and the institutions that support and legitimize all of these. Problems, however, arise as soon as one looks at this 'normal' picture from the perspective of those who suffer, or simply of those who are deprived of the basic things in life. Institutions that make up our society as a whole will soon have to be problematized as more and more of their ill-effects or unfavourable consequences are seen to affect millions of inhabitants of poorer nations.

Amidst the glut of goods is a multitude of poorer people (seeking fulfilment/gratification) who are unable to get hold of potentially gratifying commodities. Instant gratification offered by the market is real for the rich but distant for the poor.

This is not to say that instant gratification is beyond the reach of the poor; it is reachable, but in tiny measures and only with a few items. Affluent societies sell many of their commodities in regular containers or bundles to their citizens who have the capacity to pay. In affluent societies, cigarettes are sold in packs, soy sauce is sold in bottles, butter and margarine are sold in bigger parcels, or food in whole servings. In poorer countries, cigarettes are also sold by sticks, soy sauce is sold by tablespoonfuls, butter by spread or food in tiny portions. Where I come from, chicken extremities like feet (fondly called 'Adidas') and head ('helmet'), even their entrails ('IUD'), are barbecued and sold on the streets for the common citizen to enjoy, while those with more ample resources could regularly visit Kentucky Fried Chicken or MacDonald's. Such a disparity of capacity and enjoyment of resources further illustrates the meaning of class division. This fact qualifies the slogan 'class struggle', not as a fight over goods but as a distress-causing condition that further heightens the difference or estrangement between rich and poor. From this perspective, instant gratification is a distress-inducing fact for the many poor people if the poor themselves regard goods as desirable. It is unlikely that the poor masses would think otherwise, since they are part of the majority who also patronize the market. It is rare to see people who refuse to be captivated by the aggressive advertising campaigns of the market handlers. Aggressive promotions maximize means to manufacture consent. Challenging these aggressions is like crying in the wilderness, especially when consumer activists are such a rare breed and are often marginalized.

Liberation from instant gratification

If these reflections are right, the task of liberation from instant gratification is a component of that greater task of liberation from the constraints imposed by the normal capitalistic market operations.

While some citizens of the world could look up to their cash resources to realize the promise of instant gratification or fulfilment, people of poorer nations depend on meagre resources for their own brand of gratification or fulfilment. However, other groups are relying on other means to face their numerous problems. One of those groups whose activities are fired by the vision of liberation is that of the basic ecclesial communities. Found in most poorer nations, these are the cradle and home of many forms of liberation theology.

Not too many persons of the poorer nations could take advantage of the steps taken by groups of Christians who compose and organize the basic ecclesial communities. There is a promise of gratification in such associations which mainly promote popular ways of shaping many alternative forms of faith expressions in people's lives; these are expressed through liturgical celebrations, social services, self-help projects, protest actions and other activities which stress the importance of the non-monetary values of solidarity and community. The gratification offered by the basic ecclesial communities is not the same as that offered by the market producers and investors.

In the activities of the basic ecclesial communities we encounter long processes of struggle which distinguish people's waiting-in-patience disposition from the impatient urge of many consumers. Moreover, people do not merely hope for the instantaneous availability and gratification offered by commodities but also for the more enduring values of Christian compassion, kindness, etc. This can be realized only through creative participation and group celebrations in political, economic and cultural processes which directly affect their lives and the church. There are many things one can expect from such processes, but they are to be obtained without the capitalistic mode of the market, which engenders division, individualism, personal instantaneous gratification and competition for exalted ephemeral values like youth, prestige, wealth and the like. The promotion of solidarity (not division), co-operation (not manipulation), patience (not aggression), cohesion and participation (not efficiency and consistency in financial accounting), informality and warm-heartedness (not formality and indifference), sympathy (not strict price-fixing) – all of these, and many more, are experienced as gratifying by people who lead lives informed by the values that Jesus of Nazareth himself promoted.

In this connection, the monetary character of transactions (especially work) carried out in a market society will have to be a primary consideration of basic ecclesial communities, to further a vision of a community worthy of its promise to make present the reign announced by Jesus.

We can identify here the role that Christians could take as prophets and bearers of a culture which orientates people to what is more wholesome and liberating. If the basic ecclesial communities are the main venue where values antithetical to instant gratification are to be promoted, then the whole issue of upsetting the normal operations of a market economy is in order. In the basic ecclesial communities, roles, institutions and structures must develop progressively to counter the negative consequences of normal market transactions. The presupposition is that to counter the normal operations of the market (which are inimical to disadvantaged poorer persons), a normalized operation of a system based on Christian compassion and solidarity must be realized. Embodiments of counter-roles and counter-institutions can only have the effect of gradually bringing about a counter-culture which is desirable and Christian. Work and products will now be seen in a new light. The dynamics of production-acquisition-gratification will have to be met by the constancy and endurance of production-sharing-liberating praxis of the disciples of Jesus.

Instant gratification could really be a false need, after all.

Instant gratification as an offer of the market and an orientation of subjects should bring to mind the Trojan horse and the city that is about to fall.

Notes

1. See Ignacio Ellacuria and Jon Sobrino (eds), *Mysterium Liberationis. Fundamental Concepts of Liberation Theology*, Maryknoll 1993.
2. The concepts condition and determination could clarify further what is happening here. Repetitive cultural and social patterns have the effect of conditioning subjects into ways of feeling, believing and acting that further validate or reinforce

such patterns. Situations or ways of acting in work-places, for example, could shape workers into agents whose ways are more congenial to the preservation of the *status quo*. When conditions in the work-place become unbearable, resentment or resistance may arise among workers. But no matter how much they abhor the negative situation (in the absence of reforms), they usually stick to their jobs out of necessity. In this sense, the structure of work becomes a real determination. The former conditioning facilitated an individual's socialization and positive orientation or outlook towards what is perceived as one's own world. However, the more positive conditioning may not be totally indispensable when structures are accepted as necessary, because in the latter case, people would not have a choice. They will be forced to accept the rules imposed and the resources granted. The kind of conditioning process here may now become getting used to what is determining, no matter how harsh it is. This is not to say, however, that all determinations are negative ones.

3. Economists have branded the group of poorer countries with the euphemisms 'underdeveloped', 'developing'. Today, these countries are called 'emerging markets'.

The River and the Mountain

Subhash Anand

The search for instant gratification is one aspect of a highly technologized consumer society. Technology brings about acceleration: fast and abundant production, fast food, fast communication, fast transport. With abundant pornographic materials, psychedelic drugs, pop music and dance, luxury hotels, CD-ROMs, etc., the possibility of instant gratification has increased. While Asia is not adequately industrialized, it feels the impact of the technologized consumer society, thanks to the trans-continental network of communications exposing TV viewers to the latest in the consumer market. This brings about not only a cultural neocolonialism but also an alienation from traditional ethical and religious perspectives: intimate human encounters are being replaced by superficial gatherings with a thick icing of consumerist glamour, and our youth is being sucked into a cesspool of fast 'love' and fast 'dump'.

Disillusioned by this pseudo-culture, some in the West are turning to Asia for enlightenment. Unfortunately, many have not abandoned the defective paradigm: they want instant liberation! This came as a windfall for some Indian so-called gurus and bhagwans with their posh ashrams, who further dehumanized them by exploiting the gullibility of the frustrated Westerners.[1] But Asia has a solid tradition that still shapes the lives of many and can be a source of real enlightenment for contemporary humans.

Saṃsāra: the futility of instant gratification

Basic to Asian consciousness is the fact that humans experience existence as fragmented by time and space. This awareness finds its conceptualization in the Hindu doctrine of *saṃsāra:* cycles of birth and death. The word *saṃsāra* is derived from the prefix *sam* (together, conjointly) and the root *sr* (to flow),[2] and so it suggests a continuous flow. To be in time means to constantly die and be born again.[3] We are part of this universe which is constantly on the move, and so it is appropriately labelled *jagat*, a word derived from the root *gā* (to go).[4] Buddha is reported to have said 'Everything is momentary,' and therefore 'Everything is painful'.[5] It is precisely because everything here is passing away that any kind of attachment is bound to bring us sorrow. Novelties may hold our attention, but only for a short time. Indulging in things that bring us instant gratification may keep us happy for a while, but in the long run it is bound to lead to boredom and frustration, which in turn may lead to depression and even suicide.[6]

This insight is brought out powerfully in a story found in the great epic of India.[7] A king, as a result of a curse, became old overnight. His desire for pleasure, however, was unabated. So he requested his sons to exchange their youth with him, so that he could continue a life of pleasure with young women. All except the youngest refused to do so. Even after a thousand years of pleasure, the king was not satisfied. Realizing the futility of it all, he returned the youth of his youngest son, and as a reward for his devotion made him king in his place. Thus the story serves to tell us that the craving for pleasure is such that it cannot be overcome by giving in to it. This message is made explicit in a verse that we find in a related variant: a fire only becomes bigger if we pour some clarified butter on it. So too passion becomes stronger if we give in to it.[8] This story is the nucleus of a major Indian novel, *Yayāti*, by V. S. Khandekar. Explaining its genesis he says: 'I do not know if I would have written this novel, if in the decade 1942–52, I had not been witness to the strange happenings in the world and in our country – the strange spectacle of physical advancement and moral degeneration going hand in hand.'[9]

The Hindu and Buddhist sages realize that as long as we continue to be in time, we are bound to experience pain. Hence they long for freedom not merely from ethical evil (sin – as is the Christian concern), but more fundamentally from temporality itself. Already the *Bhagavad-gītā* speaks about *mokṣa* from the cycles of birth and death (7.29), i.e., liberation from *saṃsāra*. The Buddha propounded the doctrine of *nirvāṇa*, 'the complete stopping of craving'.[10] The verb *nir-vā* suggests the act of blowing out (a flame or a fire), and so the word *nirvāṇa* is evocative of the extinguishing of the constantly flickering flame of time.[11]

This awareness that human life has more to it than this world has to offer is also part of the Jewish and Islamic consciousness. The pious Jew is aware that the whole of creation is God's gift. He expresses his gratitude to God for all his blessings in the prayer after meals. But he is also aware that '[t]he nourishment of his meal is a foretaste of the nourishment of the Messianic time, just as the joy of the wedding is a foretaste of the Messianic rejoicing. Still, it is not the Messianic time, so Israel finally asks not to depend upon the gifts of mortal men, but only upon those of the generous, wide-open hand of God.'[12] If creation, gift of God as it is, cannot fully satisfy the pious Jew, much less can the instant gratification made available by technology. Hence one Jewish sage begins his book with the exclamation: 'Vanity of vanities, says the Teacher, vanity of vanities! All is vanity. What do people gain from all the toil at which they toil under the sun?' (Koheleth 1.2–3).

The Muslim believes that '[o]ur essential self is our timeless I sandwiched, imprisoned even, in our time-dependent capsule of body and enveloped by our swirling thoughts and emotions'.[13] When humans forget their true identity, they 'do not contribute to – and do not even understand or attempt to understand – the long-range moral goals of human endeavour. They are content to live their lives from day to day, indeed, from hour to hour: "they are like cattle, indeed, worse . . . they have hearts but cannot understand, they have eyes but cannot see, they have ears but cannot hear" (Qur'ān 7.179). Thus the major religious traditions of Asia see human fulfilment beyond this life. Hence the quest for instant gratification is a dehumanizing process.

Satsaṅga: the joy of being-in-communion

This Asian awareness finds symbolic expression: the river is symbolic of human existence, while the mountain reminds humans of their goal. A river is constituted by flowing water (*saras*), and this word too is derived from the root *sr*.[14] Hence every river is *sarasvatī* (having a flow).[15] It is very significant that the most sacred river of India is called Gaṅgā – a name derived from the root *gam* (to go),[16] for she is constantly on the move, and in her journey towards the ocean she is accompanied by Yamunā, who is 'regarded as the sister of Yama',[17] the god of death, and death is a powerful reminder of the futility of our existence if there is no beyond. '[T]he Buddhist [too] compares existence to a river,' and this comparison also holds good 'concerning the stream of consciousness'.[18] The Jewish exiles express their deep longing for their home while sitting on the banks of the rivers of Babylon (Ps 137.1).

On the other hand, the height of a mountain inspires awe, and its peak comes to symbolize the divine presence. This explains why we have many popular pilgrimage sites situated on the top of a hill. However there is a deeper insight: the mountain is solid rock and so it is immovable (*acala*). God too is *acala*.[19] He is beyond the vicissitudes of *saṃsāra*, beyond the ups and downs of time and space. The popular Hindu god Śiva is known as one who not only rests on a hill but also is the lord of the mountains.[20] It is on Mount Sinai that Moses encounters God (Ex 13.3). It is on Mount Horeb that Elijah hears the gentle but powerful voice of God (I Kings 19.8–13). Muhammad received his first revelation in the cave of '*Ḥirā*, a desert hill not far from Mecca'.[21] His last sermon was on Mount Arafāt.[22] The river often naturally makes us think of some hilly region, for all rivers have their origin there. We come from God and, as such, we are beings unto Being. The river is symbolic of the pilgrim character of our existence. Does this mean that there can be no moments of deep joy while we are here on this earth? The Christian message answers this question positively by bringing out a deeper dimension of our pilgrim character.

Jesus too was a pilgrim. His life in a very profound manner makes visible the mystery of the divine Word. In his Gospel, John tells us that the Word is *pros ton theon*, constantly moving towards God (1.1).[23] Jesus too is constantly moving towards his Abba, whom he encounters not only when he steps into the flowing waters of the Jordan (Luke 3.21–22), but more often in the silence of a hill-top (Luke 6.12) and it is in one such experience that he has a foretaste of his final pilgrimage (*exodos*, Luke 9.28). This journey of Jesus is precisely to the Abba, who is Love itself (I John 4.8). This Love addresses us and calls us into existence.[24] Hence our existence is grounded in Love, and so we are pilgrims not merely to Being but to Love. It is the experience of this Love that can bring us deep joy while we are still in our exile. The definitive experience of Love – a communion of three persons – can be anticipated through our being in loving communion with others here on earth, for all creatures are sacraments not only of Being but also of Love.

The call to communion is foundational to Asian religious feeling. The Hindu tradition invites us to *sat–saṅga*,[25] the Buddhist to *saṅgha*,[26] the Muslim to the *umma*,[27] while the devout Jew sees brotherly communion as the anticipation of full life on Mount Zion (Ps. 133). While the three latter traditions define communion in terms of believers, the Hindu *sat-saṅga* does not entail the confession of a particular creed, not only because *sat* denotes being in general, but also because it points to a person who has transcended narrow boundaries.[28] We can understand this concept in five different ways, depending on how we write it.[29]

We are called to communion with nature: *sat-saṅga*, to enjoy its beauty. This becomes all the more important for modern urbanized human beings. In our overcrowded cities, with their towering sky-scrapers and pollution of various kinds, there are many who have never experienced the beauty of a sunrise or a sunset, who have never felt the sounding silence of a forest, who have never seen the nocturnal splendour of a fully visible sky, who have never enjoyed the song of the birds nor witnessed the dance of butterflies. The earth is our mother, and without constantly experiencing her mothering presence we will not be fully human. Communion with her makes us whole.

As we have already noted, the quest for instant gratification is part of our technological culture characterized by acceleration. In such a culture individuals become very important, but in the process their dignity as persons becomes secondary. They are important to the extent that they promote production, provide instant pleasure or have the money to procure it. But the call to love and be loved grounds our very existence, and we become persons to the extent we love and are loved. *Sat-Saṅga*: human relations are the most concrete experience of loving and being loved. This explains why the neo-Pentecostal groups are attracting large numbers: they promote fellowship, attracting people even from non-Christian communities.[30] When we encounter persons who have a depth within them, we experience joy, and we too are challenged to explore the depth within us.

As persons we are all called to contemplative prayer (*SAT-Saṅga*),[31] to experience in some way the Supreme Being (*SAT*) already here on earth. This experience anticipates our final loving union with Love (*SAT-SANGA*).[32] Persons who have had this experience go through moments of deep joy, a joy that shapes their lives, healing them and making them more loving and caring, enabling them to reach out to heal others. Their very presence brings us peace and joy.

Our communion with nature (*sat-saṅga*), with other humans (*Sat-Saṅga*), and with God (*SAT-Saṅga*) calls for a communion with ourselves (*Sat-saṅga*), for three reasons. First, we are conditioned by our culture, religion, education, family situation, etc. We easily take on a personality that is more in accordance with popular expectations. This danger is all the more real today as we live in a scientific world that is characterized by a consumer boom and the proliferation of media which effectively manipulate us and shape our thinking. We think we are free, but so often that is an illusion, because the real motives of our actions emerge from our subconscious.

Second, God, the supreme artist, does not repeat himself. Hence every finite being, but in a very special way every human person, is his unique creation. Each one of us has a very special vocation. For this God has given us different talents. This vocation is written into our being from the moment of our conception. But as we grow in life, different layers of experience begin to cover us and obscure our vision. The unique seed that God created remains buried under many layers of soil. It does not sprout and bloom. We do not really become what God wants us to be. We do not tap all the resources latent within us. We do not listen to the depth within us. So many of us today are not comfortable with silence, but it is only in silence that we can encounter our true self and joyfully say with Mary: 'the Mighty One has done great things for me' (Luke 1.49). It is only when I really love myself and can see and accept myself as I am that I will be able to love others and see and accept them as they are.

Third, the call to contemplative prayer demands that we go deep into ourselves. God is not out there. He is present in the cave of our hearts. No doubt, the beauty of nature, the love of people around us and our common prayer bring us in contact with God. But when we encounter God in the depth of our hearts, we come to the realization that he is our depth, and that we become fully what we are meant to be only in him. We exclaim with St Augustine: '*Deus est intimior intimo meo.*' The more we realize our true self, the more joy and peace we will have – a joy and peace which the world can neither give nor take away.

Dharma: promoting communion as authentic religion

In the *Bhagavad-gītā*, Krishna tells his disciple that whenever there is a crisis of *dharma* he manifests himself (4.7), and all his activity is directed towards the maintenance of the universe (3.22–24), holding it together (*loka-saṅgraha*, 25). Traditionally, *dharma* is seen as that which sustains this universe.[33] Just as the Jewish society was held together by the Ten Commandments, so too the whole creation is held together by God's ten words.[34] The word religion – one possible translation of *dharma* – is derived from the Latin *re-ligare* (bind back) or from a hypothetical Indo-European *re-lig/re-leg* (be concerned).[35] Thus we may say that the function of authentic religion is to hold all creation together. For a believer, creation is in fact interrelated. Religion consists in accepting this and shaping one's life accordingly. This attitude finds its best expression in love.

The history of Christianity shows that the emphasis on orthodoxy has brought about many divisions in the church. It has also generated a lot of violence. For Jesus orthopraxy was more important. In the parable of the Good Samaritan, he makes it clear that reaching out to the wounded – not only humans but also the rest of creation (Rom. 8.21–22) – is a higher form of orthopraxy than temple liturgy (Luke 10.29–37). Without this forgiving and healing love our acts of piety have no value (Matt. 5.23–24; Mark 11.25). In the parable of the Last Judgment, he mentions effective concern for the needy neighbour as necessary and sufficient to qualify us for his kingdom (Matt. 25.31–45). John even seems to suggest that it is brotherly love expressed in humble service, rather than the Lord's Supper, which is the true memorial of Jesus (John 13.1–15, 35). I believe that we will be able to mediate the Christian message effectively in a society dominated by a search for instant gratification if we make our lives an effective expression of love (John 17.20–23).

Love is a boundless mystery, for God is love. It invites us to make our life a pilgrimage, a journey beyond all boundaries. Jesus was such a pilgrim. He begins his pilgrimage by entering the river Jordan. His public ministry provides us with ample evidence that his whole life and teaching was 'a challenge launched . . . at civilization's eternal inclination to draw lines, invoke boundaries, establish hierarchies, and maintain discriminations'.[36] His pilgrimage culminates on Mount Calvary, where from his pierced heart flows a river of living water (John 7.38; 19.34). That was the river of love – the Holy Spirit – that inundates our hearts (Rom. 5.5; John 7.39). This love invites us to be like Jesus: we too are called to cross boundaries and foster communion (*Sat-Saṅga*), building small communities not merely of Christians but of all people of good will, working together to heal our society and our planet. This, I believe, is a vision of hope for the twenty-first century.[37]

Notes

* I am grateful to my colleagues, Dr G. Lazar and Dr R. Rocha, who helped me to find the necessary documentation with regard to Islam and Buddhism. However, I am solely responsible for the views expressed in this article.

1. For a satirical presentation of this phenomenon see Gita Mehta, *Karma Cola*, London 1990.

2. V. S. Apte, *A Practical Sanskrit–English Dictionary*, ed. P. K. Gode and C. G. Karve, Poona 1957, 1594.

3. For a more detailed discussion of the pilgrim character of humans, see Subhash Anand, 'Tīrthayātrā: Life as a Sacred Journey', *Vidyajyoti Journal of Theological Reflection*, 61, 1997, 669–92.

4. Suyrakanta, *A Practical Vedic Dictionary*, Delhi 1981, 295.

5. A. Verdu, *Early Buddhist Philosophy*, Delhi 1985, 11.

6. In the introduction to her novel, Mehta says that our age 'is characterized by speed. Speed, being the enemy of reflection, will spread fantasy with such velocity that humans, in their pursuit of escape, will ultimately destroy themselves' (G. Mehta, *Karma Cola*, n. 1).

7. *Mahābhārata*, Poona 1933–71, Book 1, chs 70–88. For a detailed analysis of this story, see Subhash Anand, *Story as Theology: An Interpretative Study of Five Episodes from the Mahābhārata*, New Delhi 1996, 33–70.

8. Book 1, variant 693. Translation my own.

9. V. S. Khandekar, *Yayāti*, trans. Y. P. Kulkarni, New Delhi 1978, 7.

10. Verdu, *Early Buddhist Philosophy* (n. 5), 2; see also 175–85.

11. Apte, *Practical Sanskrit–English Dictionary* (n.2), 919. Hence some scholars think that *nirvāna* is total cessation of being, but this is a misunderstanding. See F. H. Cook, 'Nirvāna', in C. S. Prebish (ed.), *Buddhism: A Modern Perspective*, Pennsylvania 1978, 133–6.

12. J. Neusner, *The Way of Torah: An Introduction to Judaism*, Encino, CA [2]1974, 27.

13. F. A. Rauf, *Islam: A Search for Meaning*, New Delhi nd, 44.

14. Apte, *Practical Sanskrit–English Dictionary* (n. 2), 1654.

15. The suffix *vat* (feminine *vatī*) indicates possession.

16. Apte, *Practical Sanskrit–English Dictionary* (n. 2), 641.

17. Ibid., p. 1306.

18. A. Govinda, *The Psychological Attitude of Early Buddhist Philosophy and Its Systematic Representation according to Abhidhamma Tradition*, London 1961, 129.

19. Apte, *Practical Sanskrit–English Dictionary* (n. 2), 28.

20. *Mahābhārata*, 14.8.16; 62.13; 64.2.

21. Mohammed M. Pickthall, *The Meaning of the Glorious Koran*, New York nd, x.

22. Ibid., xxvi.

23. M. Zerwick and M. Grosvenor, *An Analysis of the Greek New Testament*, Rome 1984, 285.

24. In the account of creation (Gen. 1.3–2.22) we have the words: 'God said . . .' ten times.

25. S. Anand, *The Way of Love: The Bhāgavata Doctrine of Bhakti*, New Delhi 1996, 157–81.

26. Verdu, *Early Buddhist Philosophy* (n. 5), 146.

27. F. Rahman, *Major Themes of the Qur'ān*, Minneapolis 1980, 145.

28. Anand, *The Way of Love* (n. 25), 8–9.

29. Sanskrit does not have the distinction between capital and small letters.

30. P. Parathazham, 'The Challenge of Neo-Pentecostalism', *Vidyajyoti Journal of Theological Reflection* 61, 1997, 309, 314.

31. S. Anand, 'The Universal Call to Contemplation', ibid. 41, 1977, 414–18.

32. Anand, *The Way of Love* (n. 25), pp. 208–16.

33. Apte, *Practical Sanskrit–English Dictionary* (n. 2), 855.

34. See above, n. 23.

35. *Webster's New World Dictionary*, London 1962, 1228b.

36. J. D. Crossan, *The Historical Jesus: The Life of A Mediterranean Jewish Peasant*, New York 1991, xii.

37. I am referring to T. A. Kleissler, M. A. LeBert and M. C. McGuinness, *Small Christian Communities: A Vision of Hope for the 21st Century*, New York 1997.

Aesthetic Existence and Christian Identity

A Possible Form of Christianity in an Experience Society

Michael Bongardt

Søren Kierkegaard would not have needed to be asked twice to discuss our theme. The man who struggled so earnestly in his time and against the church of his time over the appropriate form of Christian identity would certainly have given his evaluation of aesthetic existence yet again (assuming that he was able to overcome his deep-seated discontent about 'the press'). But he would not have been concerned to give a positive definition of the relationship, as I am in the following reflections. Rather, he would have attempted to convince us once again that the earnestness of Christianity requires of us a decisive move from that life-style which he describes as 'aesthetic'.[1]

Precisely because they seem to be so vehemently opposed to our concern here, to begin with first of all I shall consider Kierkegaard's theses on the relationship between aesthetics and Christianity. They will form the critical background against which further considerations have to be expressed. Once this has been sufficiently illuminated, we shall turn to today's prosperous societies in which – according to Gerhard Schulze's analysis – the orientation on experience is extremely important. Christians seeking an appropriate life-style cannot and must not evade this aesthetic moulding of society. Rather, I shall argue, there is a possibility of recognizing the post-modern experience society in a critical way as an opportunity for finding a perceptible Christian identity.

Don Juan in constant search of the next erotic adventure; the petty-bourgeois intent on his rest; the potentate desiring power and riches; the sceptic in love with his depression – these people who at first sight seem so different are, according to Kierkegaard, united in their common goal. They are all in search of enjoyment.[2] And in order to find it they often turn to obscure objects of their desire. These may – like the loves of Don Juan, like the money to be accumulated – lie in the outer world. Alternatively – like the beauty which is vainly cherished, or the gifts which are arrogantly put on show – they may be counted among the objects which are in extreme danger and the next moment could be lost for ever. However, for Kierkegaard the real problem of aesthetic existence does not lie in the disturbing volatility of its object. What is more serious is the fact that human beings lose themselves in their striving for enjoyment, that they allow themselves to be determined by the wishes that they long for and only achieve in a transitory way. For they start by assuming that enjoyment can give their life form and content. However, those who hope to find their identity in this way are not only permanently threatened by the despair of loss but always already live – albeit unconsciously – in despair. Those must be said to be in despair who fall short of the possibilities of human existence, who refuse to be what they could be out of anxiety or a lack of seriousness.[3] Thus the people presented to us by Kierkegaard are united not only in their striving for enjoyment but also in the basic character of their existence. They are not themselves, not independent, but dependent on their wishes and thus on the fragile aims of their desire. In short, they are desperate.

According to Kierkegaard, there is only one way out of such despair over the aesthetic existence orientated on enjoyment: the resolve of the individual to be himself. In the resolute adoption of my own freedom I overcome my dependence on the fleeting objects of my enjoyment. Only in this choice does what appears outside it only as a paradox become understandable: by accepting that I am desperate, I overcome my despair. For now it no longer dominates me: instead of succumbing to it, I can once again relate to my wishes – regardless of whether or not they are fulfilled. I do not gain my identity in the fantasy world of unlimited enjoyment, but only in the recognition of the possibilities, offers and limitations within which I have the opportunity and responsibility to shape my life.[4]

Kierkegaard knows that the choice which he calls for represents a great venture. That it is necessary for a really human life can remain permanently hidden in the apparent security of aesthetic life; it can be refused out of anxiety about the open spaces to which it leads; above all, if it is ventured, it can sink into grief about one's own past, which is now recognized as a guilty falling short of one's own possibilities. The more clearly Kierkegaard perceives these dangers, the more his conviction grows that the choice of self can succeed only as a religious, indeed a Christian act. Only in trust that their guilt is already forgiven, that they are accepted with his limitations, may human beings choose themselves as what they are.[5] Only in this way can they find the freedom to which they are called. But even this promise which is necessary for the successful step to freedom encounters us in a paradoxical form which causes scandal. The promise of forgiveness that encounters us in Christ, in the figure of the God-man, calls for the recognition that as sinners we need this gift.

Kierkegaard accuses the church of his time of concealing the seriousness needed for this step. For the sake of the gospel and human beings it is necessary to speak out against a society and church which take it for granted that their petty-bourgeois life of enjoyment is Christian. Kierkegaard saw himself called to make this protest and thus turn Christendom back into Christianity.[6] For him, part of this call was to renounce the many forms of aesthetic existence which stand diametrically opposed to the life of a Christian. In it human beings refuse the choices that lead them to freedom.

With some justice, Kierkegaard is constantly accused of having directed his undisputed analytical perspicacity too closely to the phenomena of a bourgeois society and church.[7] In fact there are no reflections in his writings on the remarkable fact that none of the figures whom he criticizes – or he himself – ever had to think about their material livelihood; they took for granted an abundance of possible pleasures. It is no coincidence that he makes Nero the prototype of aesthetic existence. For this Roman emperor had almost unlimited wealth and power.[8] And we also look in vain in Kierkegaard's sermons and polemical writings, which certainly are not lacking in sharp rebukes, for an accusation against social abuses, a view of the blatant distress outside bourgeois securities. This fighter for Christianity remains at a remarkable distance from the social and economic reality of his time.[9]

150 years after the death of Kierkegaard this reality has changed significantly in the highly-industrialized countries of Western Europe and North America. The cultural sociologist Gerhard Schulze gave his widely-noted analysis of West German society at the end of the 1980s the significant title *The Experience Society*.[10] After ten years stamped by far-

reaching political and social upheavals, Schulze's results doubtless need to be modified. But regardless of this, his insights have not ceased to be illuminating for the present day. Schulze agrees with most comparable investigations that while the division of society into different social strata orientated on income has not simply been done away with, it has markedly lost significance. His observation that closed and self-contained milieus are increasingly losing their contours and dissolving cannot claim any originality either.[11] The remarkable feature of Schulze's analysis, rather, is his thesis that after the collapse of these structures which shaped European modernity society does not prove to be an amorphous mass. We can recognize the rise of new milieus. These milieus no longer differ – as did the classical social strata – by the extent to which it was possible within them to satisfy needs. What the individual 'can achieve' is of only limited importance for his belonging to his milieu. Similarly his ideological position is of subordinate interest. What is decisive, rather, is the quality of the experiences which are sought and offered in the individual milieus.[12]

Some want the thrill of bungee-jumping, while others prefer the repose of the coffee bar. Unprecedented crowds fill newly-built museums, while others prefer to sit in front of the television if they are not trying out the most recent roller-coaster at the fair. And in this quest for specific qualities of experience, individuals are not concerned only for themselves, as might appear. For a long time now group milieus have formed in which not only shared events are looked for, but individuals are recognized or repudiated by their own choice of events. So after the end of the former structures, the need for social location and orientation is not frustrated, but finds new satisfaction. Belonging to a particular milieu becomes an essential mark of identity for individuals and relieves them of the pressure to live their life in loneliness. The specific milieu to which one belongs can be recognized by a system of codes understood and recognized by all. Small variations in clothing, the choice of transport, turns of phrase used in passing can be recognized without much difficulty. Out of these Schulze constructs five milieus of experience to which individuals belong and to which they are happy to be assigned.[13] Anyone who wants to belong to the 'niveau milieu' will report at length his last visit to an art preview, but fail to mention that the previous evening he enjoyed watching a soap opera on the television. And no one who hopes to be recognized by the members of the entertainment milieu will appear with a philosophical book rather than the latest comic.

The necessary presupposition for this remarkable change in social structures is an economic shift: the experience society owes its rise to the change from a society of shortages to a society of prosperity.[14] Where this change has taken place, according to Schulze, we can see a significant change in strategies of selling and advertising. As long as money is short, customers attach importance to the most functional and durable products. Once this basic lack has been overcome, other factors become criteria in deciding what to buy. Now cigarettes are on offer which promise freedom, soap which smoothes the skin, and cars with which one can overcome the force of gravity. A number of products are on sale which are no longer distinguishable in usefulness and quality of material, but which are distinguished in advertising by markedly different qualities of experience.[15] Items which formerly had a place in a corner of the general store – toilet paper, chocolate and sun glasses – now fill whole divisions of department stores or supermarkets. The customers would be hopelessly overloaded with this oppressive multiplicity, were it not that here again the milieus guide them. The milieus indicate what kind of bread and what sort of holiday suits me, what experience on sale I should take up.

A society with such a structure almost completely leaves aside the fact that the prosperity that it presupposes is by no means as taken for granted and universal as it likes to suppose, but is available only to a minority.[16] The number of those who have no alternative other than to wage daily, often vain, battle for their survival is growing – and not just outside the states which define themselves as prosperous societies. Kierkegaard's understanding of aesthetic and moreover of Christian existence was, as I have indicated, open to the charge that it was focussed too much on what was then a narrow sector of the prosperous middle class. If the scheme of a relationship between social conditions and Christian identity which I shall go on to work out does not want to be open to the same charge, it must be concerned not to lose sight of this scandalous injustice.

However, first of all it is necessary to finish this analysis of the 'experience society'. It is capable of functioning only on one condition: all who live in it must have adopted the imperative on which this new economic and social structure is based. According to this the meaning of life to be striven for lies in successful experience: 'Experience something! Experience yourself!'[17] Anyone who is ready to follow this requirement will easily believe the promises of a market orientated on experience and be prepared to be shown the direction by them. And if appearances are not deceptive, this readiness is widespread in Germany and in other Western societies. Therefore skilful marketing can easily relieve the individual of the decision what experience to seek, how and when. The products and qualities of experience that they promise change increasingly rapidly.

A bridgehead opens up: Kierkegaard's critique of aesthetic existence seems predestined to encounter protestingly the society analysed by Schulze. For what do we find in the now considerably enlarged circle of the prosperous who have prescribed for themselves the quest for experience, if not the aesthetic striving for enjoyment which was a characteristic of those prosperous citizens described by Kierkegaard? And do not those who join in the experience market in fact not only lose their money but also the awareness of their freedom, their selves, their possibility to choose? Certainly every day the market offers a wealth of products from which the customer has a 'free choice'. But as a rule care is taken not to draw attention to a quite different possibility: individuals could take the freedom at least partially to avoid this hunt for experience, and once again to be free from the dynamic which seeks to dominate them.

So there are plenty of voices from Christian, church, circles warning against the new form of society which has come into being. There are complaints about the lessening interest in church and community work, the rapidly declining number of churchgoers, the allegedly decreasing readiness to take responsibility and accept ties. All these phenomena are thought to be evidence for the thesis that Christian identity is in principle incompatible with a recognition of post-modern society, that the experience society leads to a dissolution of Christianity.

In the face of this apparently clear criticism of a life-style that Kierkegaard describes as aesthetic, and is far more widespread today than it was in his time, is it not vain, indeed presumptuous, to seek a positive relationship between aesthetic experience and Christian identity?

At any rate, on close inspection it appears that the supposedly unanimous complaints of Kierkegaard and the representatives of today's churches are in fact diametrically opposed to each other. Behind the current church criticism of the present-day world there is often disappointment at the collapse of the confessional milieu, those social residues in which bourgeois existence and unquestioning church membership came together to produce allegedly Christian identity. So the complaint is over the loss of that church phenomenon which Kierkegaard so resolutely repudiated. Looking at the invitation to make a decision of faith in seriousness and freedom which is issued by the Bible and has been constantly emphasized by the church tradition, we can hardly reject Kierkegaard's opinion. Furthermore, it is clear from this perspective that the social changes, which are also momentous for the church, are making a major contribution towards overcoming a form of church socialization which has become questionable.[18] Obviously that does not of itself mean that they are also constructive in forming a Christian identity. Not least Kierkegaard's repudiation of aesthetic forms of existence is opposed to that.

If we are to pass a sufficiently differentiated verdict here, we need to look at the basic insights of modern philosophical aesthetics. This can help to show up Kierkegaard's limitations in his account of aesthetic existence and to overcome them. In this way we can see the goal that Kierkegaard set himself but never reached: the aesthetic quality of a Christian existence.[19]

Philosophical aesthetics understands itself to be a comprehensive theory of perception.[20] And its decisive modern insight is that human perception is never a purely receptive act, but is always essentially active interpretation and formation.[21] The impressions of the senses do not lead to a faithful copy of the outside world in human consciousness. Rather, people form the impressions of the senses into the picture that they make of them. Such a formation takes place against the horizon of existing patterns of understanding and goals that have grown up both individually and collectively. The same is true for any attempt to express ourselves. To show what we think, feel and intend we have a variety of possible signs from which to choose. But that means that any way in which we relate to ourselves and our environment is already dependent on the possibility of our freedom. All our perceptions, all our statements, are grounded in the freedom in which we give them form. Therefore Kierkegaard's understanding of the aesthetic existence does not go far enough: it describes only those who are not yet aware of this freedom which is already the basis for all their quest for identity. Because of this narrowness Kierkegaard leaves out an important aspect of human freedom: human beings remain dependent on sensual, perceptible communication in their lifelong task of realizing their freedom, becoming themselves. Only by means of such symbolic communication can human beings be reached by the world around them and can they reach that world in turn.[22] Therefore human existence always has an essentially aesthetic stamp. There can be no question of leaving this stamp behind. The important thing is to use it for an appropriate realization of identity which is grounded in freedom.

Because and insofar as Christian faith knows that human beings are called to respond to God and shape their lives in freedom,[23] these insights of aesthetics have a far-reaching significance for the quest for an appropriate form of Christian existence.

This importance is already evident when facing the event proclaimed by the church as the revelation of God.[24] According to the Bible, God gave his concern for human beings a variety of tangible forms. Among these, according to the Christian confession, the life and fate of Jesus has unique, unsurpassable significance (Heb. 1.1f.). Just as convincing as Jesus' unconditional dedication to the kingdom of God which he preached was the overwhelming Easter event witnessed by the disciples. But even these events – like any other objects of perception – are not clear in themselves. Only in the act of free assent in faith are they seen as the appropriate, unique form of the love of God. The same is true of the observation of 'signs of the times' required by the gospel (Matt. 6.3). These too call for an interpretation if they are not to remain ambivalent and thus meaningless.

It is not just the way in which God shows himself to human beings that has a symbolic character which respects freedom. Believers also face the task of giving their faith a tangible form – a form which they shape and find in their identity. So looking for the aesthetic form of Christian existence involves far more than the 'appropriate' furnishing of a church building, a liturgical celebration or even a parish magazine – important as these ways of communicating content may be. First and foremost it is important to give a face to God's concern for human beings in which Christians believe, to make it tangible. It will remain an important part of this concern to bring to the eyes and ears of those who are in danger of shutting themselves up in enjoying their prosperity the distress which calls for help and a change in political and economic structures.

Those who are aware of this challenge will no longer pass sweeping verdicts on the social changes that I have described. In any case the possibility of such a repudiation remains questionable: after all, even supposedly dropping out of the experience society goes with a particular quality of experience. Kierkegaard perceptively also accused the pessimistic sceptic of enjoying his solitary attitude.

The alternative to such an unperceived ambivalent relationship to the conditions of a post-modern prosperous society that cannot be changed at will is a critical recognition of its limitations and possibilities. There is no disputing the fact that an 'experience market' can develop a dynamic which leads to a Don Juan's senseless quest for adventure. The rise of new amazingly closed milieus leads to new difficulties in understanding. Beyond question there is a danger that the prosperous society will cynically barricade itself against the distress of those at whose expense it lives. The experience society as a rule shows itself to be helpless in the face of sickness and death.[25] All this may be the case, but the changed society also offers an unsuspected variety of aesthetic figures, of possibilities of perception and expression. This multiplicity extends from the immense technological possibilities of discovering and relieving the need of others, through the countless occasions for intercultural exchange, to the opening up of areas in which people can try out new forms of binding and loving life together. These new possibilities are extremely important for a worthwhile humane and thus also for a Christian existence. For this already became clear in the analysis of the experience society. In seeking and choosing specific experiences human beings predominantly express their need to be seen and respected, to give and find recognition.

Therefore to shut oneself to the variety of aesthetic possibilities which have grown up not least because of this need would be as inappropriate as uncritically to affirm the social *status quo*, which all too often is stamped by blindness and contempt. Rather, there is an opportunity to make use of this new spectrum of perception and expression that has grown up in order to help people to become aware of this freedom. Where this awareness has been aroused and people have resolved to take responsibility for one another, they can face the domination of an experience market orientated on profit – and also the traditional expectations of behaviour cherished by the churches and stamped by a bourgeois confessional milieu. They will then independently seek and choose the appropriate symbols of loving care, not least to make the victims of these society feels respect and dignity. In such a resolute and level-headed recognition of forms of present-day life, Christian existence can take on an aesthetic form which can be perceived; and it calls for a decision either to reject or accept the testimony of Christian men and women in freedom.

Translated by John Bowden

Notes

1. Cf. Kierkegaard, *Writings about Himself* (SV XIII, 529–33); in what follows reference will be made to the definitive complete Danish edition, *Samlede Vaerker*, Copenhagen 1900ff. The main translations contain references to this pagination.

2. Cf. Kierkegaard, *Either/Or* (SV II, 163).

3. Ibid. (SV II, 173f.).

4. Ibid. (SV I, 187–95).

5. This is the result of the dissuasions of the obstacles to the successful personal choice which Kierkegaard adduces in his pseudonymous works. It is described for the first time at length in Kierkegaard, *Unscientific Postscript* (SV VII, 507–11), and then compressed in id., *The Sickness unto Death* (SV XI, 127f.).

6. Cf. especially Kierkegaard, *Exercises in Christianity* (SV XII, 54–58).

7. This accusation is made most urgently by Theodor W. Adorno, *Kierkegaard: Konstruction des Ästhetischen*, Frankfurt [2]1974.

8. Cf. Kierkegaard, *Either/Or* (SV II, 168–70).

9. There is little justification for the charge frequently raised against Kierkegaard of a solipsistic anthropology. Rather, we find in him important beginnings of reflection on the dialogical and sociological constitution of human existence, even if these are not developed sufficiently. Cf. Bongardt, *Der Widerstand der Freiheit*, Frankfurt 1995, esp. 74–90, 190–207, 297–315.

10. Gerhard Schulze, *Die Erlebnisgesellschaft. Kultursoziologie der Gegenwart*, Frankfurt am Main 1992.

11. For locating his approach in sociological discussion cf. ibid., 78–91.

12. For his basic thesis cf. ibid., 34–78.

13. For the evidence and significance of the orientating sign cf. ibid., 184–6. For a characterization of the five elevated milieus of experience cf. ibid., 277–333.

14. Cf. ibid., 34f.

15. Cf. ibid., 427–31.

16. For the marginalization of problems by the experience society: Schulze mentions not only poverty but the destruction of the environment, ibid., 657–71.

17. '"Experience your life" is the categorical imperative of our time', ibid., 59.

18. For a positive assessment of these phenomenon of a new departure see Karl Gabriel, *Christentum zwischen Tradition und Postmoderne*, QD 141, Freiburg, Basel and Vienna 1992, 163–202; Medard Kehl, *Wohin geht die Kirche?*, Freiberg, Basel and Vienna 1995, esp. 39–48.

19. Cf. Kierkegaard, *Either/Or* II (SV II, 161).

20. For what follows, cf. Brigitte Scheer, *Einführung in die philosophische Ästhetik*, Darmstadt 1997, 53ff.

21. Ernst Cassirer introduced into philosophical epistemology the concept of 'forming' which is used here and in what follows. In this way he succeeded in broadening the classical philosophy of transcendence so that it became a comprehensive theory for the human understanding of the world. Cf. Ernst Cassirer, *The Philosophy of Symbolic Forms*, Vol. 1, New Haven 1953.

22. For the necessary symbolic communication of human freedom cf. Thomas Pröpper, *Erlösungsglaube und Freiheitsgeschichte*, Munich [2]1988; also Bongardt, *Widerstand der Freiheit* (n. 9), 104–6.

23. For the philosophical interpretation and responsibility of Christianity see Pröpper, *Erlösungsglaube* (n. 22).

24. Hans Urs von Balthasar, *The Glory of the Lord*, Vol. 1, *Seeing the Form*, Edinburgh 1983, above all kept pointing to the importance of aesthetics in perceiving the figure of Jesus.

25. For the last mentioned danger cf. Armin Nasehi and Georg Weber, *Tod, Modernität und Gesellschaft. Entwurf einer Theorie des Todesverdrangung*, Opladen 1989.

IV · Ecclesial Praxis: Challenges, Opportunities, Models

Decline or Transformation of Solidarity?

Norbert Mette

I. Changing forms of solidarity

The joint message from the leading bodies of the two great churches in German (the Council of the Evangelical Church in Germany and the German Bishops' Conference) on the economic and social situation in Germany, published in 1997 and composed with the broad participation of various church and social groups, contains a notable section under the programmatic title 'Opportunities and Forms of Solidarity in a Renewed Social Culture'.[1] It contradicts the widespread prejudice that the rapid process of individualization – noted in the loosening of traditional ties with the milieu and the replacement of an orientation on existing norms with obligations entered into by personal choice, and thus the increases in possible options – is to be identified with a lack of solidarity and individualism. It is correct, the document states, that the awareness of being bound together in solidarity is now being taken less for granted. But it would be short-sighted to seek to derive this from a total decline of solidarity. If one looks more closely, what can be noted is not a decline but a change of solidarity.

This new 'way in which solidarity is practised and lived out' is discussed in further remarks in the section. It is described more closely as increasingly taking place through 'voluntary bonding together in solidarity in groups, which often come into being through a shared commitment to a common cause'.[2] The next section continues:

> This common cause relates to new values. Women and men today often seek to realize aims in life which formerly seemed excluded.

They may combine paid work and honorary positions, family and profession, personal free space and political commitment. They are concerned to develop as creative and unconventional personalities, and to take responsibility in a society. They want to think globally and act locally. Moreover new values to orientate on have spread through society, e.g. those relating to matters of the environment and of gender. Common to many of these new value orientations is an extension of the understanding of solidarity. Dangers and risks which have become boundless in extent and degree in principle affect everyone, and therefore call for an awareness of global interconnections. This universalization of solidarity differs from earlier and more limited forms of solidarity.[3]

In detail, without any claim to completeness, a list is given in section 159:

Thus in the West of Germany over the last twenty-five years civic initiatives, new social movements, welfare associations and other non-governmental organizations have enlivened the debates in politics and in so doing opened up ways towards a reorientation of state action. In East Germany the peaceful revolution was possible only because social groups, often allied with the church, worked against the totalitarian state and round the table at the time of transition developed a democratic culture in which those involved looked for new ways in solidarity and co-operation. In East and West, groups concerned with development policies have been amazingly persistent in emphasizing that responsibility in solidarity is universal and cannot be divided. Initiatives with the unemployed have sought socially meaningful work which would not otherwise have been done. Church communities, church groups and associations have implemented actions of solidarity. *Ad hoc* civic committees have organized chains of light in which the solidarity of the majority of the people of Germany with threatened foreigners has been expressed. Groups related to the environmental movement and the women's movement have tried out new life-styles and model forms of community in solidarity over and above their political commitment. Moreover thousands of new self-help groups have come into being. Church communities, church institutions, organizations and initiatives have taken part in such searches and developed new forms of voluntary and full-time involvement. In both church welfare associations more than a million women and men are engaged in voluntary roles.[4]

This brief text is remarkable, not least because it contains none of the lament which for some time has been current in church and society, to the effect that there is a steady decline in solidarity – even going so far as to say that the increasingly rapid trend towards individualization sparked off by modernization will inevitably end up in a 'society which has abandoned solidarity'.[5] More sophisticated analyses lead to other findings, which can be summed up as follows.

1. There are different forms of solidarity which have developed under different social conditions and which in the course of social change are challenged either to go along with the change or to decline. Thus – following Karl Gabriel[6] – one could speak of ties and obligations of solidarity which grow out of relationships of kinship or neighbourliness, and these differ from the relationships of solidarity based on rank in a feudally ordered professional world. Different again from this is the solidarity which came into being in the class society. This combined the fate of shared physical labour and proletarian existence and led to an effective fight against the exploitation endured, bringing about humane working and living conditions. The solidarity which came into being in the context of uniting the confessions, of the kind practised and propagated in the Catholic milieu from the end of the nineteenth century to the middle of the twentieth century, has yet other emphases. If the first two forms of solidarity are typical of pre-modern, traditional society, where they contribute to maintaining the given and unchangeable order, the two forms of solidarity cited after them are typical of the beginning of modernity as it established itself, and in this period served disadvantaged groups (workers, Catholics, women etc.) as a means to fight for emancipation under the slogan 'Togetherness means strength!'.

2. Present-day talk about the crisis or decline of solidarity certainly applies to many of these traditional forms of solidarity. In part they have become dispensable because other social networks have been established – even if they continue to be practised to an amazing degree, as is the case for example in the alliances of kinsfolk and neighbours. In part they have come to an end because the goals for which they fought have been achieved. In addition, as I have already indicated, some of the solidarity needed to safeguard life which grew up at an early stage when there were no alternative measures have long been institutionalized and regulated legally. Society is composed of a great many alliances to which people belong either voluntarily or of necessity – solidarity is one trend among others (hierarchical organizations, market), applied to the conditions of modern society.[7]

3. Not least, because basic security now extends virtually to the whole of the population, an awareness of solidarity and a corresponding praxis has come into being which is now sparked off by challenges and works on them, and which tackles the problems arising in the course of a process of modernization which is taking place with increasing speed. The fact that the threats and dangers which this process produces do not affect just individual groups and do not stop at the frontiers of nation states has also given a tremendous impetus to the growing awareness that all human-kind is bound up together and that we are therefore globally responsible for one another in solidarity.

4. This removal of the limits to the requirement of solidarity means that the activation of the potential for solidarity has a very different starting point from those stimuli towards solidarity which arise out of natural or social pressures for one's own survival. Karl Gabriel has described the change that the process of modernization has made to new possibilities and forms of commitment in solidarity voluntary chosen as follows:

> Under the pressure towards modernization, solidarity becomes a matter of selecting from many possible solidarities. It is chosen as part of a scheme of life which is open to changes. The bond of solidarity can fulfil the function of demonstrating something of the unchangeability of the person only if its character is emphatically voluntary. Here the demand that commitment in solidarity must be capable of being depicted at a personal and social level increases. There is a greater obligation to explain why one is committed and in solidarity with this and not with that. On the one hand the plurality of available solidarities leads to a more open and looser bond of solidarity. Changing points of reference for solidarity in the course of one's life can become an expression for changes in one's own priority of values. On the other hand, the link between solidarity and the safeguarding of personal and social identity also produces new forms of continuity and stability. Commitment in solidarity can be expected to be stable as long as it 'contributes something' in the broadest sense to the individual.[8]

The solidarity which was formerly orientated on purpose has turned into a solidarity orientated on feeling and experience.[9]

5. In this perspective it proves short-sighted to argue that the process of individualization makes it more difficult than before to activate solidarity in the conditions of present-day society. There is no evident conflict with solidarity in the possibility of a person's greater freedom to

develop his or her own individuality – which cannot simply be identified with individualism or egocentricity; rather the opposite.

If nevertheless the degree of commitment in solidarity falls short of the need for solidarity – which is hardly a new phenomenon in history – this cannot primarily be blamed on individuals who are supposedly thinking and acting only in relation to themselves. Moreover a permanent change cannot be achieved by appeals for greater solidarity, however emphatically they are made. Without wanting to deny the need for changes in personal awareness and behaviour, one must also ask questions about the predominant social structures and the pattern of rationality which underlies them. Do they further solidarity or hinder it? In this connection it is by no means a demonization of the economy to state that thinking and acting in solidarity is actually an alien body in the rationality which has become dominant in the economy, a rationality primarily concerned with increased efficiency and the maximizing of profit in ever shorter cycles of investment, with the lowest possible costs and excluding potential competition. If such economic rationality exceeds its bounds and also becomes the norm in other spheres of life, it proves to be not only disruptive but also destructive. As the statement by the German churches quoted at the beginning clearly notes: 'A society in which only merit and profit count, in which competition and power are the sole determining factors, is on the way towards surrendering humanity, solidarity and responsibility for others.'[10]

In absolutizing this rationality, the economy itself has reached the point of undermining its own presuppositions. After all, it has to refer back to qualifications or virtues like 'the capacity to negotiate shared rules, to work together in a team, to be stable under pressure and reliable in agreements',[11] or virtues like honesty, loyalty, diligence and a readiness for responsibility, without which it cannot function. But how are these to be developed and prepared without cost to the economy which expects them, if the spheres of life (family, school, etc.) which alone show the (inter-)personal, spatial and temporal presuppositions for this kind of formation of personality are increasingly being colonialized by an economic rationality?

In the meantime the insight is spreading even to economic circles that an exclusive fixation on one's own advantage at the expense of the deforming of individuals and the destruction of society and ecology ultimately also is not worthwhile economically, and people are beginning to ask whether increased co-operation is not far more effective than constant and inexorable competition.[12] However, it would be difficult to arrive at such reorientations in the economy and politics were there not more or less massive pressure from civic counter-movements – a number of which have been cited in the text of the social statement by the churches quoted at the beginning of this article – which do not want the increasing undermining of the cultural resources of social solidarity to be the last word, but are actively attacking it.

II. Education for solidarity

We need to ask urgently how people come to support one another in solidarity and do not subject themselves to the dictate, guided by specific interest, that one should be concerned only for one's own advantage.

First of all in this connection it is important to note the significance of early and therefore fundamental experiences of interaction in human development. If one thinks how dependent children are from the beginning on being able to grow up in an environment in which they can develop their various competencies in dealing with the world, with others, and with themselves, step by step, according to their stage of development, the demands aptly made by Ursula Peukert under the postulate of 'solidarity between the generations' are particularly important:

> Because concrete possibilities of self-development open up to the child only through the preliminary interpretation of the adult, which puts its action in the wider context of a defined social world, the child can fail to find itself. It is exposed to the superior power of the partner in the interaction and forced to adapt. The relationship between child and adult is so precarious because the adult is dominant, equipped with the advantage of knowledge and ability which the child cannot catch up with, and because the adult must bring into a relationship with the child not only his or her possibilities, but also his or her limitations and hurts. However, if the adult attempts to reflect on this asymmetry with the child and to change it into an 'inter-generational reciprocity', the child is recognized as a partner on an equal footing and thus the communicative presupposition is created for a development in which the child can learn for its part to recognize others as others. Only a solidarity with the next generation which has this structure opens up the possibility of growing into humane forms of social life and appropriating them.[13]

It follows from this, as Ursula Peukert warns us, that this responsibility of the older generation for the younger generation must not just be individualized, but must show consequences, to the point of shaping the whole community.[14]

In general, the formation of an identity with a strong self which is thus really capable of relationships proves to be an indispensable presupposition for action in solidarity – an identity which is capable of meeting new challenges from others and open to questions, thus becoming involved in a constant process of learning, which is far from being conflict-free.[15] Personality types who are full of anxiety, obsessive and narcissistic are hardly capable of solidarity; after all, the risk of personal disadvantage is bound up with action in solidarity. In positive terms that means that personal maturity, a healthy self-esteem, openness, freedom from anxiety, a capacity for dialogue and conflict, a readiness to share and to give things up are, among others, central characteristics of a personality type which is capable of commitment in solidarity and prepared for it; such commitment is usually sparked off by a concern which grows out of empathy for the concrete other who comes into view, reinforced by a sensitivity to that other's suffering. According to G. M. Prüller-Jagenteufel, the following characteristics may be cited as special marks of this action and the attitudes which guide it:

> A perceptiveness and a sense of justice, i.e. not only the rational recognition of a situation of need or oppression, but similarly the existential involvement which springs from allowing oneself to be affected;
> . . . a realistic sense of the possible which on the one hand offers protection against utopian dreams and fantasies of omnipotence, yet finds the capacity to set off for new shores in with a lively imagination and spirituality;
> . . . courage for active co-operation in social action against need – not through the paternalistic giving of alms, but as far as possible on the same level. Here it should be noted that where suffering cannot be removed, it can be diminished by sharing it.[16]

Here too it becomes evident to what degree practice in solidarity can be hindered or even prevented by social structures which militate against it. So it is inadequate merely to want to portray and practise solidarity merely as an individual virtue; undeniably combined with it is the demand for a transformation of society as a whole in the direction of the realization of democratic culture in all spheres of life. This alternative society which no longer isolates and deforms its individuals is taken a step further in those groups, initiatives and movements which in their concrete projects for and with people nearby or far away, and also in the way in which they shape their own common lives, attempt to practise solidarity and thus help one another to overcome the resignation that so easily arises, especially in isolated commitment: the feeling that nothing has a purpose.

III. Church(es) as a force for solidarity?

As is clear from the lists of solidarity groups and movements mentioned in the statement with which this article began, a considerable number of such groups has settled in or near to the churches. We could see this as a confirmation of the thesis that traditional religion so far has clearly shown a particular power leading towards solidarity. This is supported by a study which, though carried out in Austria, has produced findings which are significant at least for the greater part of Europe. It has demonstrated empirically a greater degree of solidarity than average in the context of religious networks.[17] However, by way of qualification it must be said that this was the case only where religion or more precisely Christian faith could be experienced as creating freedom and encouraging relationships. By contrast, a religion felt to be authoritarian shapes those personality types, already mentioned which are incapable of solidarity.

This leads to friction when both religious types meet within the church(es); many of the church or Christian solidarity groups have a sorry tale to tell about this. Above all when they do not merely limit their commitment to the charitable relief of need in the traditional sense, but have also learned to note and take seriously its political references, they quite often find themselves forced to the periphery of their own church communities. A study of the self-understanding and praxis of Christian Third World groups in the Catholic Church of Germany has provided abundant evidence of this.[18] That makes all the more remarkable the assessment of these groups made by the authors at the end of the study. They can be transferred to other solidarity groups in the church's sphere.

The 'Third World' groups are small ('radical') minorities within the church and on its periphery. But they have revived social Catholicism and confronted it with the 'international social question'; on their way – occasionally on the periphery of the church or even outside it – they have a task of pastoral sanitation. In addition they are voluntary, and involve the expenditure of a great deal of time and energy; they are the leaven in a solidarity which is lived out and provide the impetus towards a change of awareness in the ego-societies of the North without which one world in solidarity cannot come into being. The ethic of global responsibility ('think globally') must come into being below ('act locally') so that it can move something above.

The investigation supports this assessment of the Third World groups as elements of a society capable of solidarity and empathy. The church authorities have not yet discovered this creative potential and therefore have criminally neglected it. The groups need more recognition and support than they have received so far, of both a non-material and a material kind. They are relieving the church of a good deal of the work for international justice required of it by *Populorum Progressio* and *Sollicitudo Rei Socialis*. If the church wants to take its commitment to international justice as a world church seriously, it must fundamentally rethink its relationship to the active posts of this commitment.[19]

Instead of lamenting a decline of solidarity in society, the churches themselves therefore have occasion to examine critically their own capacity for solidarity.[20] They will understand everything else as incidental and keep to their prime concern to the degree that they learn to see the core of Christian faith as a praxis of universal solidarity grounded in mysticism, and do their utmost to make it reality as far as possible – with a view to the challenges of society and those in their own ranks.

Translated by John Bowden

Notes

1. Cf. *Für eine Zukunft in Solidaritat und Gerechtigkeit. Wort des Rates der Evangelischen Kirche in Deutschland und der Deutschen Bischofskonferenz zur wirtschaftlichen und sozialen Lage in Deutschland*, Bonn and Hannover nd (1997).
2. Ibid., 64.
3. Ibid., 64f.
4. Ibid., 65.
5. Cf. P. M. Zulehner (ed.), *Vom Untertan zum Freiheitskünstler. Eine Kulturdiagnose anhand der Untersuchungen, 'Religion im Leben der Österreicher 1970–1990' – 'Europäische Wertestudie – Österreichteil 1990'*, Freiburg, Basel and Vienna 1991, 84–8.
6. Cf. K. Gabriel, 'Guter Rat tut not! Christliche Gesellschaftsethik und die Suche nach neuer Solidarität', in *Sonderbeilage zu 'Einsichten 1996' des Oswald-von-Nel-Breuning Hauses*, Herzogenrath 1997.
7. Cf. F.-X. Kaufmann, 'Solidarität als Steuerungsform – Erklärungsansatz bei

Adam Smith', in id. and H. G. Krüsselberg (eds), *Markt, Staat und Solidarität bei Adam Smith*, Frankfurt am Main and New York 1984, 158–84.

8. K. Gabriel, 'Guter Rat tut not!' (n. 6); cf. also id., 'Krise der Solidarität', *StdZ* 14, 1996, 393–402; id., A. Herth and K. P. Strohmeier, 'Solidarität unter den Bedingungen entfalteter Modernität', in ead. (ed.), *Modernität und Solidarität*, Freiburg im Breisgau 1997, 13–27.

9. Cf. G. Schulze, 'Jenseits der Erlebnisgesellschaft. Zur Neudefinition von Solidarität', in *Gewerkschaftliche Monatshefte* 45, 1994, 337–43.

10. *Zur wirtschaftlichen und sozialen Lage in Deutschland. Diskussionsgrundlage für den Konsultationsprozess über ein gemeinsames Wort der Kirchen*, Bonn and Hanover nd (1994), 51f.

11. U. Peukert, 'Solidarity between the Generations', *Concilium* 1996/2, 76–85: 84.

12. Cf. F. Hengsbach, *Abschied von der Konkurrenzgesellschaft*, Munich 1995.

13. Peukert, 'Solidarity between the Generations' (n. 11), 82.

14. Cf. ibid., 84; ead., 'Der demokratische Gesellschaftsvertrag und das Verhältnis zur nächsten Generation', *Neue Sammlung* 37, 1997, 277–93.

15. For what follows see G. M. Prüller-Jagenteufel, 'Unfähig zur Solidarität?' *Diakonia* 25, 1994, 237–46.

16. Ibid., 245; cf. in more detail also id., *Solidarität – eine Option für die Opfer*, Frankfurt am Main 1998, esp. 453–73.

17. Cf. P. M. Zulehner et al., *Solidarität: Option für die Modernisierungsverlierer*, Innsbruck and Vienna 1996.

18. Cf. F. Nuscheler et al., *Christliche Dritte-Welt-Gruppen. Praxis und Selbstverständnis*, Mainz 1995.

19. Ibid., 423; cf. also K. Gabriel and M. Treber (eds), *Christliche Dritte-Welt-Gruppen: Herausforderung für die kirchlicher Pastoral und Sozialethik*, Bonn 1998.

20. Cf. O. Fuchs, 'Solidarität und Glaube', Deutscher Caritasverband (ed.), *Caritas '99. Jahrbuch des DCV*, Freiburg 1998, 19–35; H. Peukert, 'Universale Solidarität – Verrat an Bedrohten und Wehrlosen?, *Diakonia* 9, 1978, 3–12.

New Affective Communities and the Problem of Mutual Understanding

Diana L. Hayes

Is it possible for the Christian church to serve as a prophetic voice for the future in a society which looks upon institutionalized religion and faith in a being or power outside of oneself as a sign of weakness? How can it relate to the new forms of affective community which have arisen in response to the growing secularization and privatization of religion in the United States? Is it possible for constructive dialogue to take place, not only within the churches themselves, but with those who have left or have never fully been a part of it? Can the Black church, as presently constituted, and a womanist understanding of church and community, serve as a paradigm for bringing about and furthering this dialogue, thus providing a strengthened future for the Christian church?

The once and future church

American Christian churches have failed in their mission to build community based upon faith in Christ in contemporary society. The blame lies partially within themselves, increasingly fragmented by internal battles over identity, doctrine and practice, and also with contemporary American society, a product of Enlightenment ideals of human autonomy and rationality. Christianity has lost much of its authority today. Many, including Christians, are engaged in pursuing material wealth, supported by an ethos of individualism and the subsequent privatization of faith. The result is the absence of a Christian moral voice within public and private arenas. Many Americans now base their decisions not on what is good or just for all but on what is good for themselves alone. They have lost a sense of God or a higher power external to themselves and rely, as a result, solely on their own instincts and basic human nature to guide their everyday lives.

As the nation grows increasingly technological, materialistic and consumeristic, we ask: are the US Christian churches capable of claiming a publicly spiritual voice? Will they be able to survive into the twenty-first century and grow in influence as a viable source of identity and community for Christian Americans in the face of increasing competition from other religions and non-religious sources as well?

The mainstream Christian church is in danger of becoming irrelevant, if it is not already. There are several reasons for this. First, there is the growing exodus of educated young adults (twenty to thirty-five) who formerly made up a significant proportion of their population. Most mainstream churches today, regardless of racial or ethnic make-up, contain the moderate to conservative middle class, who still find their identity in being Christian and see the church as a source of community and well-being. Unlike the more radical-right churches who have retained this group, the educated youth of contemporary society, with more liberal views, find themselves increasingly stifled in churches which are unable to recognize or utilize their intelligence and education. The church is seen as reactionary, attempting to resist contemporary culture rather than participate in it in a transformative way. Many 'boomers' have turned away from the ethic of 'self-denial' which served prior generations and provided a foundation for church membership to an ethic of 'self-fulfilment' which emphasizes the enjoyment of life as opposed to sacrificing for a better afterlife.

Thus, many of the newly emerging affective communities attract them because they still hunger for a place where they belong, where they can find solidarity and community. Christianity is no longer seen as being capable of providing that place. Other religions and spiritualities now attract them, especially those labelled 'New Age', as well as cultural and civic organizations which provide many of the services the church once provided: education, counselling, entertainment, socialization and an outlet for social welfare, without the sticky strings of allegiance to a particular way of being, thinking or acting.

These new groups can be as simple and unstructured as reading and Bible study groups, sports and fitness clubs and associations, and other purely social gatherings, or more complex in the sense of New Age religious groups such as Wicca, mixtures of Eastern religions and philosophies and new sects and cults which seem to offer community and solidarity. Other groupings are based on sexual orientation, physical situation, and political/social world-view. They range in size from a handful, including 'house churches', to mega-churches, but all serve the purpose of providing outlets or ministries in which persons can engage themselves fully or partially, as they see fit.

Secondly, as noted, many of the services once seen as specifically religious in nature, such as religious education, religious identity and social welfare, are now being provided by other entities. Religious education has become the domain of secular colleges and universities, which treat religion as simply one of many other social constructs to be observed and discussed but not necessarily participated in. Counselling, employment opportunities, therapy, training in social values and the provision of various benefits have all been, in many ways, relegated to civic associations and governmental bodies, although the latter are now in process of disengagement. Private organizations provide health care, treatment for social dis-ease, housing, employment training and other services. They do so devoid of the Judaeo-Christian ethic or any other religious norms which formerly served to ground these actions in a moral stance in which a loving but judging God played a paramount role. Para-church groups now provide opportunities for community as well as para-liturgies adapted to the particular beliefs of their followers, often without reference to the church itself. The church has become a referral system rather than a place of lifelong attachment.

Third, individualism has fostered a privatization of religion and religious life, often aided and abetted by the churches themselves with their dualistic emphasis on the sacred realm in opposition to the sin-full secular world. The latter is ignored or rejected as a locus for Christian activity, while the former becomes the only mission of the church, losing sight of the balance which Jesus affirmed in the Great Commandment and the Great Commission. Many Christians choose, not surprisingly, to opt out of institutionalized religion in its entirety, seeing it as having no meaningful bearing on the lives they are actually living. They turn instead to a more personal spirituality, which too often makes God merely a personal deity answerable to them and they to God.

Fourth, the US has become the most religiously pluralistic and racially/ethnically diverse country in the world. This further serves to relegate institutionalized religion to the background of one's life as people gather in ethnic and racial groupings, across religious lines, to develop communities which they believe serve their needs better. The church's inability, increasingly evident, to respond to these disparate voices and perspectives hinders its appeal and ability to evangelize especially those who make up the rapidly growing population of peoples of colour. The church must ask itself if it is possible to 'find vision and identity in its present muddle of confusion and low morale, and commit itself to the diverse groups that make up this society'. To do so, the Christian churches must shed their austere, judgmental, authoritarian, transcendent image which stifles dialogue and seeks only agreement at any cost. Such an image does not fit the world-view of most Americans regardless of the end of the political spectrum on which they find themselves. Nor does it allow for the human nature of the church itself, with its constantly changing composition of people from all walks of life, all races and ethnicities and all cultures. Nor does it not fit Jesus' own beloved community. It must reach out to those who have remained faithful, Christians of colour and women, but feel marginalized and ostracized by their fellow Christians and their church leaders.

The Black Christian church

The Black community in the United States can serve as a paradigm, for these problems cross denominational, racial, ethnic and gender lines. Historically, persons of African descent, wherever they found themselves after the diaspora of the Atlantic slave trade, have been a people with a strong faith in a transcendent, 'wonder-working' God who created them and encouraged them to flourish, looking out for them in good times and in bad and helping them to survive. That God was also immanent in their lives, walking among the people, dispensing grace and blessings on the deserving while chastizing and challenging those who went astray. African Americans had an intimate personal experience of God that was also communally grounded and affirmed.

Ironically, this faith which moved mountains has been increasingly pushed to the sidelines now that slavery and the legal apartheid of Jim Crow have seemingly been laid to rest. As doors to colleges and universities, corporate and political offices, and formerly segregated suburbs have been opened, we are confronted with a form of 'black flight' which has left a decaying inner city and its inhabitants, predominantly Black, to fend for themselves. These newly enfranchised and increasingly wealthy Blacks have also chosen to opt out of organized, institutional religions, choosing instead to look within themselves and to those with whom they interact for support and spiritual guidance. Others have turned to new faiths, including Buddhism with its more individualistic philosophy of life, and Islam, as well as to evangelical forms of Protestantism and charismatic Catholicism. Still others flock to non-denominational mega-churches open to varying expressions of faith.

Why these shifts? A major reason is the negative association that many African Americans still have with Christianity. Since it is as a religion that fostered, encouraged, and supported the institution of slavery throughout the Americas, many want to shed all memories of that period and the religion attached to it. Others feel that the Black church has abandoned its former liberative and radical stance in its efforts to become mainstream. Its message of other-worldly bliss and this world passivity is not one they want to hear. Too many Black churches, while rejecting the distorted Christianity imposed upon African Americans which supported their dehumanization, have, however, continued to foster the dualistic world-view which sets greater store on a heavenly salvation than on transforming contemporary society into the kingdom of God. At the same time, they deny their liberationist origins by condoning sexism, classism and homophobia in their communities. As a result, just as in other Christian churches, young and educated Black adults, as well as those abandoned to lives of drugs, disease and despair in the urban core, have abandoned Christianity as a false religion which perpetuates rather than challenges the myriad forms of oppression presently existing in the US. The more the churches privatize their faith, the less contact they will have with contemporary society.

The search for community

Paradoxically, many Americans are seeking a return to a place they have never really known, one of security and comfort, a community of understanding in which they feel supported and affirmed without the overshadowing threat of condemnation or guilt. Historically, religion provided the answer to that longing, serving as a place of safety and refuge from the constant buffeting of the outside world.

Religion was the great modifier, balancing extremes of wealth and poverty, knowledge and illiteracy, and even male and female leadership roles. Everyone had a position and place within the church. This was especially true for two groups in the US, African Americans and Roman Catholics, segregated by the rest of society for being different, yet, through their own system of religiously-based schools and churches, able to educate and prepare their children for a more inclusive future. The church was everything and provided everything, supplying all needs, whatever, their nature, and affirming their members' human dignity and self-worth.

Today that easy egalitarianism is missing in most Christian churches, as people come together for other reasons, usually divided by race and class, as well as gender and sexual orientation. The mainstream churches, seen as enclaves of the elite, are unwelcoming. Many react to what they are experiencing by retreating to what seems to have been a better time in a non-existent past, while others simply abandon ship, seeking out those churches or other forms of community where they feel comfortable and affirmed rather than isolated.

Womanist theology as public theology

. . . (A) public theology seeks to overcome the cultural marginal . . . character of contemporary theology. It seeks . . . to contribute to the upbuilding and critical transformation of our public life. It refuses to remain confined to a private sphere, dealing with issues of personal spirituality, salvation, and ethics.[1]

Womanist theologies seek to counter such isolation, providing new understandings of both theology and the role of the theologian in both church and the wider society. They seek to ground their 'doing' of theology, which is seen as not merely an activity of the educate elite, in the experiences of those marginalized. Theology is seen as more than the interpretation of scripture and dogma. It serves as a source for the creation and reconstruction of beliefs and dogmas, enabling the theologian to serve as critic and constructor of tradition rather than passive interpreters only. Thus theologians serve as mediators of knowledge and conduits for the interchange of knowledge at all levels. Womanist theology, which seeks to overcome the multiplicative oppressions of race, class and gender, while rebuilding community across confessional lines, serves as a public theology which unites rather than divides. It serves as a public voice for all in its efforts to create a holistic world in which all forms of marginalization and alienation are eliminated. A womanist public theology would have to engage confessional truths, but to do so, at least within Christianity, in ways that allow for the diversity that exists within the body of Christ. It would also, however, have to engage other public voices, religious and non-religious, in order to participate in the transformation of this world and to prepare for the coming of the next.

A womanist vision of church and community

Is this then the answer? How can it be otherwise possible for mainstream churches to influence the shape of the future if they are not where their people are? Do they have the vision and identity necessary to respond to the increasing parochialism of American society, which is manifested in the midst of a growing diversity, or will they continue to bog down in internal strife which resolves nothing? Will Christians increasingly embarrass themselves by fighting with each other in public and hand over authority to secular institutions because they themselves can reach no agreement resulting in the loss of core teachings about love, forgiveness, fellowship and redemption?[2]

As people move into communities both within and outside the church which speak directly to their specific needs, the gay/lesbian community, charismatics and evangelicals, fundamentalists, new age spiritualists, wiccans and non-denominationalists, the Christian church must look within itself to uncover those faults which are pushing people away while recovering what is central to their faith and serves the needs of their faithful.

Black Christians, again, while certainly suffering from many of the same problems, can provide answers. Some of the largest and most active Christian churches in the nation are those with a predominantly Black membership, yet open to all races and ethnicities. They seem able to offer a welcoming community which provides identity and belonging, while inspiring their members to open themselves up to those greatly different from them, those marginalized like themselves from society as well as those who once were their oppressors. Their services are lively, emotion-filled extended celebrations of the greatness of God not simply in the far-off future but in the here-and-now. The needs and concerns of those present and absent are addressed through a variety of service and ministry programmes which pull the members out of their insulated worlds and into the lives of those perhaps less fortunate or greatly different from themselves. They serve as a bridge that enables people from diverse cultures and backgrounds to come together and form new communities of shared faith which also empower them to make positive contributions to the betterment of society at large.

Perhaps they, and other similarly thriving churches, are successful because they have been able to bring to life affective relationships which can overcome difference and 'otherness' that would normally fragment community. William James noted that 'Our judgments concerning the worth of things, big or little, depend on the feelings the things arouse in us.' We have too often accepted society's and the church's dualistic dichotomies which separate rather than unite. Instead of seeing difference as divisive and the 'other' as a threat, should not the church be engaged in working towards overcoming difference? Such a church recognizes that the gospel begins with the people where they are, rather than requiring them, often with a loss of culture and identity, to commit to the church before they have experienced it in its fullness. They base their worship and community life on relationships, as Jesus did, providing a place of fellowship and friendship which then opens one's heart to accept faith in Christ. They work to challenge the stereotypical vision of some human beings, recognizing that God is all things to all people (I Cor. 1.22) and we are all of us in our diversity the children of God.

Such churches seek to change the way in which we, as human beings, interact with our fellow human beings. For we are too often blind to the needs and feelings of those who are different from ourselves. In order to overcome this blindness, the values upon which we base ourselves must be addressed in such a way that we can acknowledge that these new groupings are legitimate in their own right and that we can learn from them if we are open to dialogue with them. Their values go beyond self-fulfilment to an effort to re-engage in the life of the world rather than to withdraw from it. As a result, they move away from individualistic and materialistic consumerism to community and the sharing of life in responsible and meaningful ways. These values are in agreement with Christian values and need to be developed and more widely shared. However, we are able to share the values of another group or culture only when we remove the barriers that prevent us from seeing and feeling from their particular perspective. This shift can only take place when we are able to change how we feel about someone or something. Thus, having feelings about or towards another is legitimate when those feelings shed a new light on the experience of the 'other' that we have had. Once one is able to feel differently, one is also able to see differently. Because of the ability to see differently, one is able to judge differently and, finally, to evaluate differently. The result of this change of feelings makes it possible to be towards a people or culture in a totally new way.[3]

It is this new way of knowing which the Christian church must encourage and itself engage in, institutionally, locally and individually. One who is able to be open to the feelings and attitudes of others, or some particular situation, is exposed to the possibility of being able to feel another's inner secret. 'Feelings are thus seen to build a bridge between the particularity of the life of the senses and the illuminative awareness of intellectual insight. They form a link between contact with the concrete and understanding the universal . . . Each must be faithful to his own opportunities. But each must also respect those of others. Each must recognize that it is through feelings that he is awakened to value.'[4]

In the United States, the value of feelings has been deadened or denied. Nothing interests or surprises us as each catastrophe or grotesquerie is hyped. Nothing moves us to feel, especially in another's place, resulting in an inability to understand them as they truly are, rendering them hopelessly 'other'.

In a society where one's every desire is seen as legitimate, and satisfying those desires is valued more than their possible impact, negative or positive, on others, mutual understanding can only come about when we are able to put ourselves into another's place and recognize their spirits as kindred to our own. As Christians, we are still unable to do this; how can we then engage in dialogue with and attain mutual understanding with those who do not profess the Christian, or any other faith?

Womanist theology's effort to build community across racial, ethnic, gender, sexual, and class lines serves as a viable avenue for overcoming the myriad divisions which still plague US society and the body of Christ. As a newly emerging theology of liberation being done by women of colour who have, historically, been oppressed by all, it provides a unique voice as yet untainted by the limitations of other theologies. It attempts to cross racial, class, gender, and sexual barriers as well as denominational lines to form solidarity amongst all which can be transforming. Their commitment to community calls forth the memory of the early church's emphasis on community, one holistic and egalitarian. Womanists recognize that to build such a community requires that we listen to and hear the voices of those once marginalized in US society and those who have been dominant, that we learn from each other and that we work together to bring about much needed change in our churches and our world. A womanist vision of church envisions a healing and holistic community grounded in a shared faith yet open to new 'ways of being church' which invite and foster mutual understanding among those seeking a faith which can 'move mountains' in their lives and the lives of others.

Notes

1. L. E. Cady, *Religion, Theology and American Public Life*, Albany, NY 1993.
2. Robert Wuthnow, *Christianity in the 21st Century: Reflections on the Challenges Ahead*, New York and London 1993, 10.
3. James F. Brown, *Affectivity: Its Language and Meaning*, Washington, DC 1982, 122–3.
4. Ibid.

Fulfilment – Experienced for a Moment yet Painfully Lacking?

Hans Kessler

I. A look at the changed situation

First we must ask: is the trend to expect immediate satisfaction from the moment really something new in history?

(a) In his novel *A Mass for the City of Arras* (1971), Andrez Sczypiorski depicts the dramatic situation at the time of the plague in 1458, which within a short period carried off almost a fifth of the population of the city. It would afflict a person quite unpredictably, and the next moment that person could well be you. So it destroyed all order and certainty and drove people to irrational orgies, with the slogan, 'Let us eat and drink, for tomorrow we die' (Isa. 22.13). That sort of thing always seems to happen in times of crisis. It is like dancing on a volcano. Who knows what the morrow will bring? Perhaps one may be dead tomorrow, so enjoy the present moment, today. It was the same with the intellectual circles in Berlin around 1930,[1] as it was with the well-to-do in Jerusalem who are described in Isa. 22, when the city was under extreme threat. This kind of hunger for life which breaks out – for a moment – seeks enjoyment, experience in the moment, because it fears that tomorrow all will be over and experience will no longer be possible.

If these examples are of transitional behaviour in a crisis situation, in his play *Awakening Spring* (1891), Frank Wedekind deals with the problems of a youth which is to be spent in a selfishly unsympathetic, mendacious, meaningless adult world. Either one reproduces this in protest or rejects it by suicide ('I shall not enter this world'), finally to hear the discouragingly hopeless message that there is no other world than this one and that the best that remains is therefore to enjoy the delights and satisfactions which offer themselves in the moment. A world which has withdrawn into sheer immanence, with no perspectives or prospects, allows only this momentary experience of happiness. But is it really an experience of happiness? Is it not a desperate substitution for resignation and depression?

(b) What is the new element in our situation shortly before the end of the second millennium? It is not easy to grasp, even approximately. We are in the midst of a global upheaval which is taking place with violent, breathtaking speed, and with no consolidation in sight.

Now precisely this is one of the most striking signs of our time:[2] the headlong acceleration of technological developments; of the streams of capital, commodities and information; the socio-cultural change, so that it is impossible to forecast what (what hardware and software, what values, what chances on the labour market for what training, what knowledge) will be relevant tomorrow. What holds good today may already be out of date tomorrow. One cannot rely on prognoses. One can rely only on one thing: everything is in flux. Everything – the whole of society – is rushing on hectically and fatally under its own momentum, without a goal (for the 'grand narratives'[3] which promise salvation beyond the world or within it have lost their power). One must hold on and make sure that one does not drop off; this gives rise to a sense of being overdriven and overheated and being asked too much of. Everything seems to be taken up in a regime of economic process with no alternatives. This regime makes use of the needs which it generates itself, exploits them further and clothes them in the colours of the promise: advertising presents everything as an experience which can be bought. A dynamic has been unleashed globally: on the one hand it opens up more and more unsuspected possibilities for more and more people than ever before and heightens demands, but on the other hand it destroys the natural foundations of life and social ties. Thus the rising generation can get the impression that the basic mechanisms of society into which it is to be introduced are endangering its own future. Education thus contradicts itself; it reduces the readiness to make an effort and to commit oneself to wider, common interests – outside one's own group.[4] The self experiences itself as a chance product of a chance natural and social evolution, which disappears again.

However, the experience of impotence to alter overpowering trends in any way – on the one hand the problems of the future which cause anxiety (like unemployment, drugs, the creeping devastation of the environment) and the underlying panic over death, and on the other the explosive increase in material goods, the materialization of values (reinforced by the presentation on TV of worlds of luxury and pleasure gained quickly) and the expectation of finding the happiness one dreams of by devouring consumer goods and unlimited mobility – brings about a growing pressure to expect immediate fulfilment in the present without the least effort. Combined with this is a tendency no longer to wait until something is grown and mature, no longer to expect anything from a more distant or even from an eschatological future. People no longer have visions; they close their eyes to the future because in any case it makes them anxious. If things turn out badly or come to an end tomorrow, at least in retrospect one will have had 'something from life'; it will have been 'beautiful'. Somewhat wearily, but free from tension, people turn to the unchangeable in a kind of cheerful hopelessness. Present life is the only, last opportunity: get everything out of it, do not neglect to experience everything in it.[5] Even a declining standard of living will not, it seems, change this primary orientation, which runs straight through all groups of the population.

A mediaeval saying runs: 'I come, I know not whence; I go, I know not whither; no wonder that I am happy.' Luther was able to give the saying a Christian twist: 'I come, I know whence; I go, I know whither; I am surprised that I am sad.' Most people live today less from great overarching hopes and perspectives than from short-term intentions and tangible goals. 'Experience your life – now' is the imperative of the secondary culture which now spans the globe. It is enough to live life like this, in the present – without a goal.

II. Doubts, questions and impulses

(a) The basic question is: can such an attitude be maintained humanly in the long term?[6] To live like this seems to function only if the problems are suppressed as permanently as possible and one is indifferent to the needs of others. Certainly people cannot live and be happy in life without forgetting the suffering of others and the fragility of their own existence, at least for a while. Joy, festivities, happiness are part of life. But the relaxed cheerfulness of the carnival used to be followed by a reflection on one's own transitoriness: the rhythm of the seasons corresponded to the different sides of reality. Today the tendency is to blot out fragility and vulnerability, weakness, guilt and decay, suffering, ageing and dying as completely as possible. One event, one entertainment, one festival follows the next. It's enjoyable, and that's enough. That was fun! When shall we have the next one?

However, there is something desperate, something escapist, about this attitude. That emerges when the ever new-hasty fulfilment which is sought fails to materialize over a period of time or becomes impossible. If in crises in life there is no longer that which provided satisfaction, then emptiness, resignation and depression paralyse everything. It may then be that we come to realize that something in our lives is no longer in tune, that we are more than the hunger for experience.

Present-day developmental psychologists and theoreticians of culture diagnose a fragmented, disintegrated, 'empty self' which – constantly in search and fleeing from its own emptiness – all too exclusively loses itself in the external, and seeks compensation by extraversion and through satisfactions contributed from outside[7] (at the expense of the environment, the world around, posterity, the inner world). Material satisfactions repress – to a greater degree than serves life – the non-material fulfilments which find it difficult to assert themselves against the external stimuli of the world of commodities and media, because these have to be faster, louder, more inexhaustible, apparently more perfect. However, because the satisfaction communicated by these external stimuli remains superficial, new disillusionment sets in which is obsessively concealed by renewed and if possible even stronger stimuli. Always new, always more, always faster, always more fleeting.

Such an outward-directed, surfing attitude to life means that certainties and ties are now only temporary; they are no longer the backbone of life. The 'flexible person',[8] who practises self-preservation without self, often forms an identity only at particular points; this identity holds for a certain time but no longer provides a standpoint which makes detachment from what encounters it from moment to moment possible, so that in the end 'anything goes'. In a society of ultimate indifference and boredom, there are outbreaks of hatred and violence which aimlessly seek simply to break through the all-pervading indifference by pure action without feeling, to act out vital (or necrophilic) pleasure and to show one's own uniqueness and narcissistic difference.[9]

For others, the consumer, entertainment, experience society, with all its efforts to make life interesting and amusing, at some point becomes 'too much'. Satiation, superfluity and disillusionment set in, because this society in truth offers 'too little'. Like the episodes of experience which come one after another, any added sense of life from them proves to be transitory and insupportable. The (post-)modern project of self-realization and experience is beginning to exhaust itself. The suppressed experience of a more radical need, a need for redemption, is reappearing.

There is a quest for something enduring, definitive, that does not fly away, that does not become obsolete, that is not disappointing, is not put to shame. The longing for wholeness, the far-reaching, great desire cannot be stilled in the shallow waters of petty enjoyments. If it is to be fully affirmed, life needs an ultimate goal and perspective.

(b) But where today do people find orientation and support when they arrive at a critical turning point in their lives? They find it in a maze of the most diverse offerings of meaning and salvation, in which they may chance to take this direction or that, and often continue searching from one to another. Quite often, once again guided by an orientation on experience, they select from the plural offers something which on the one hand has the attraction of the new and exotic and is not yet worn out, and on the other meets their own current needs and evokes the desired psychological effects (feelings, moods, being gripped, ecstasy).[10] What is decisive is not the content of the religious offer but the stimulus of the new and the momentary sense of being caught up in it – no matter by what.[11]

In these respects, initially Christianity comes off badly. Handed down over a long period in Western Europe and amalgamated with culture, it seems discredited, worn out, outdated, no longer a source of the experience of meaning and salvation.[12] However, most people (including Christians) no longer know its sources and spiritual riches: there is something unexpectedly new and unknown to be discovered in the apparently well known. But this is not tangible, cannot be experienced quickly and without effort; it has to be discovered, to grow in the process of life.

On the other hand, isn't being gripped by an Other who is not in our control, the current experience of liberation, of being accepted, of becoming whole, and so on a basic factor for Jesus and the original Christianity? And don't Christian movements and practices related to experience take on a new attraction, which for many people is not just transitory but abiding?

Doesn't living Christianity always start from a quite decisive basic experience without which even today's individuals – thrown back on themselves in the quest for meaning and identity – can hardly be Christian any more? Wasn't Karl Rahner referring to this basic experience when he said that the Christian of the future would either be a mystic or would cease to be a Christian? What is this experience of foundation and redemption?

Many Christians, even pastors and theologians, find it difficult to answer this question. That shows how far the heart of Christian belief has disappeared from view – and from life. Perhaps this is the main reason for the decline in the spiritual radiation of European Christianity in a time hungry for contemporary, spiritual experience.

III. A perspective

We now turn to the basic experience of a firm foundation and of salvation which makes up the core of Christianity.

(a) From an anthropological perspective, behind the quest for consumer goods and experience there is a deep longing which of course cannot be satisfied in this way. Such a quest indicates a quite fundamental and ultimately infinite human need, which was formerly met by traditional religion with its message of redemption: that primal need which now, once the horizon of religious meaning has fallen away, makes itself felt in all its lack of satisfaction as the real element of unrest and insatiability. In the end it seems that human beings can be explained only in religious terms: 'You (God) have made us for you, and our heart is restless until it finds rest in you.'[13] Pascal's and Kierkegaard's analyses of existence in this direction are surprisingly topical. According to Blaise Pascal, all human beings strive for a constant basis and for happiness. But the happiness is neither outside us nor in us; it is in God, and therefore both outside us and in us. If human beings do not seek their basis and their happiness in God, then they have to seek it in themselves in a perverted way: 'He then feels his nothingness, his forlornness, his insufficiency . . . his emptiness,' and: 'There will immediately arise from the depth of his heart weariness, gloom, sadness, fretfulness, vexation, despair.' Thus all that is left for him is flight from himself (from turning to the heart, to God) into diversion and activity. 'Take away diversion and you will see them dried up with weariness. They feel then their nothingness without knowing it (viz. the real reason for it).' 'He then in vain tries to fill the inner void from all his surroundings . . . but these are all inadequate, because the infinite abyss can only be filled by an infinite and immutable object, that is to say, only by God Himself' (and then – in God – that which encounters us outside ourselves as in ourselves).[14]

Kierkegaard basically made out such existence detached from God and thrown back on itself to be anxiety. Anxiety about themselves drives individuals to cling with all their efforts to themselves and to the finite. Instead of being clearly grounded in God and thus, supported by God, being able to accept itself in all its contingency and nakedness, the self gets into a wrong relationship with itself. It is seized with unconscious despair over being-for-itself – which first become conscious in self-knowledge before God. Either it wants desperately to be itself (i.e. it attempts with all its force to justify its existence, to create duration, content and absolute significance), or it desperately does not want to be itself (i.e. it denies and repressed itself).[15]

Anxiety about contingency, the fear of death, drives modernity and its hectic activities: the anxiety of basically having no ground under one's feet and being empty, worthless, unloved, ultimately indifferent or even disruptive. Below the surface it permeates, constricts and twists the whole of life.[16] All the forms in which human beings – in so far as they do not know that they are absolute – deny themselves in depression or tenaciously seek to demonstrate that they matter (by striving for more and more possessions, enjoyment, power, influence etc.) can only momentarily reduce the deep anxiety over life. Human beings cannot achieve a real foundation and real significance – and not just pretences – in this way; their own mortality makes them seem finally completely insignificant, transitory entities if no one has the power to save them and their beloved from complete insignificance and a final negation.

In the field of practical remoteness from God, this underlying destructive dynamic of anxiety is ultimately inescapable. The basic anxiety over existence could 'only be overcome in an unconditional trust in an Absolute which is over against existence', in whose transitory absolutely human will the human being 'may himself live himself, because this Will wants him to be'.[17] Whether God can be the basis of absolute trust and therefore a real experience of salvation depends on who and how God is. Only if God is not himself terrifying (calculating, punitive, etc.), but that deeply benevolent goodness to which Jesus bore witness with his living and dying, can God – and God alone – be the foundation for that unconditional trust in which human beings free themselves from their deep-seated anxiety and are healed at the roots.

(b) The basic Christian experience indicated here can be explained by a comparison with the basic Buddhist experience. Buddhism begins from the basic experience that everything is transitory. Everything – including every state of happiness, every beloved and the self itself – is transitory and brings frustration; all desire and attachment to the transitory therefore produces suffering is full of suffering. The Buddhist way of redemption from the ocean of suffering then consists in the hard work of freeing oneself from all thirst for life, all desire and all inner ties, including that of love. Accordingly the experience of redemption consists in becoming free, in a superior tranquillity – which radiates serenity and all goodness, and ultimately in extinction, as a flame is extinguished. Only this extinction (Nirvana) in the face of all that is transitory, the perception of the absolute void, can give inner satisfaction and peace.

Where do we find the basic experience, the way of redemption and the experience of redemption in Christianity? Christianity also knows the experience that everything is as transitory as grass and shadows (e.g. Pss. 39.5–7; 102.12; 103.15f.), that all striving for sensual enjoyment as for wisdom is fleeting and vain (e.g. Koh. 1.14) and that one must become free from all desires and all self-seeking (e.g. Rom. 15.2; Phil. 2.3ff.; etc.).[18] But its basic experience – which determines all other experience – is different. It is the deep conviction and experience that in and above everything that totters and passes away there is another reality which does not totter, but rather stands and is more reliable than anything else (Ps. 90.2; 93.2, 5; Isa. 7.9b; 40.28ff., etc.). It is the experience of a reality which embraces all things (Ps. 139; Acts 17.27f.), penetrates everything to the innermost (Isa. 6.3; Jer. 23.24; Wisdom 1.7; 8.1) and – this is the decisive thing – is a 'You' full of goodness (Ps. 36.6b; 103.9 etc.), a You who is analogous to a person and transcends the personal, who is there and promises 'I am there' (Ex. 3.14; Isa. 52.6; 58.9), so that human beings may be certain that 'YHWH is my shepherd, I shall lack nothing; he leads me; even though I walk in dark valleys I fear no evil, for you are with me' (Ps. 23). This 'You are with me' expresses the basic biblical experience. This 'You' gives human beings a last point of reference which cannot be shaken, which alone gives support in all that is fleeting, to which we can hold (= Hebrew *he'emin*, belief) and on which we can rely.

To be able to rely on something presupposes the trust that we are not forsaken when we let go of ourselves (in unselfish love or – completely – in death) but rather that we are in 'good hands'. But who says that at the foundation of all transitory reality, determining it eschatologically, is a last clear good reality on which we can rely without exception? It cannot be read off the misery of the world, which casts dark shadows on the divine. Human beings, also in the Old and New Testaments, constantly project their ambivalent experiences and strivings on to God, so that God seems terrifyingly ambiguous – gracious and cruel, bringing happiness and inexorable punishment. Certainly parts of the Old Testament (e.g. Hos. 11.8f.) and sometimes other religions (e.g. in the Bhagavadgita) point beyond this ambiguity, but it is Jesus who first overcomes it with great clarity. He experienced and discovered God as the one who is pure 'goodness' and unqualified mercy (Mark 10.18; Matt. 9.7–11 par.; 20.1–5; Luke 15.11–32; cf. Titus 3.4 etc.) or – in the Johannine formulation – unconditional 'agape' (I John 4.8, 16): 'God is light (or agape) and there is no darkness (or hatred) in him' (1 John 1.5). Jesus obliterates all that causes anxiety and fear from the picture of God (cf. 1 John 4.18; Rom. 8.15) and issues an invitation to trust the primal ground of reality as that which is good without remainder (Abba): the love which is unconditional for all, to be trusted and lived from.

The goodness which is meant here[19] is not cheap or harmless. What is meant is neither the goodness which selects what is sympathetic to it nor that pathos-free tranquil goodness towards all beings which 'without an inner tie'[20] remains indifferent and equidistant from all, but the goodness which seeks a relationship and forms ties, which is interested in the concrete other for his or her own sake, and affirms them practically – in their other and distinctive character, taking the side of those who are excluded because it is resolutely for all and for a community of all without segregation. Jesus did not say simply that God is good, which would be nothing new, but asserted (with his whole existence and praxis) that God – sweeping aside all conditions and bursting all bounds – is good to each and everyone, particularly to the one to whom I am not good. He lived in this way although he experienced the harshness of the contradiction to the full and it cost him everything. He was executed by people who could not bear this boundless goodness, because they lived their false life, separating themselves from others.

(c) Jesus discloses the way of trust and goodness.[21] This is communicated in a historical and intersubjective way: whether other people can gain the redemptive trust in ultimate reality depends on the way in which we encounter them. We have responsibility for one another, and others have a right for us to show them what is most important in life:[22] that redemptive relationship to God and that redemptive dealing with one another in which the provisional experience of salvation possible in the present life (and which means a promise of full, indestructible salvation).

Those who rely on the God of Jesus experience what we need and long for most deeply. They encounter an incomprehensible goodness which loves them from the depths and accepts them for themselves, which offers a security that cannot be lost and lasts in all circumstances (come what may). As soon as it grasps them, it does not stop there but brings them on the way of goodness which leads to others to whom it applies equally. To the degree that people thus (like others) feel themselves unconditionally affirmed, they already know that they are in sheer grace completely dependent on what they make of themselves, what others make of them or what role they play with them. To this degree they need no longer fight obsessively for that fundamental confirmation, fullness and security of their own existence which everyone needs; they are more and other than their achievements and experiences, their defeats and shadow sides. Certainly they do not always have feelings of happiness, but they do rather have rather less fear for themselves and others (they even dare freely to confront the powerful). Often enough the experience of God will fade away; they will struggle with God like Jacob, quarrel with him like Job, cry out to him like Jesus on the cross, but they will not be abandoned by him (Gen. 32.26b; Job 42.3, 5; Mark 15.34): they will pray their way through again to trust. Every morning they will seek to ground themselves anew in that first foundation which gives support without being constricting, which makes flight and losing oneself in external things unnecessary. It becomes possible to deal with the things of this world in a free and easy way. This firm ground gives support and power to venture the rebellion of the good against injustice, misery and despair.

Those who attempt to live out trust in the God of Jesus and therefore goodness open up to others redemptive experiences of liberation, happiness and wholeness – even if they are only the size of a mustardseed. Only incidentally and gratuitously do they themselves get something of this experience of happiness. For the experience of happiness, wholeness and meaning cannot be manufactured; it does not come directly with reference to the self (in self-stimulation, psychology, the fitness cult and so on) but is only received unintentionally, in transit to the others (in having time for others, listening to others, giving to others). 'Whoever loves has passed over to life; whoever does not love remains in death' (I John 3.14).

It is redemptive to be able to reckon with another reality than our own. Life is given a clear orientation if sheer immanence, if the market and experience society is not the sole horizon for our living and dying within which we must be content, if the ultimate thing that can be attained is not an apersonal ground of faith, extinction, but rather an ultimate good for everyone – which itself suffers all ungoodness, and expects our goodness. Then there is the certainty that we change things, and this ultimate good will change everything else.

Tranlated by John Bowden

Notes

1. Cf. Carl Zuckmayer, *Als wär's ein Stück von mir*, Frankfurt am Main 1996, 9ff. ('A moment lived in paradise'); 365ff. ('Why then weep?').
2. For what follows cf. H. Kessler, 'Umwelt, Markt, Ethik und Religion', in Gerd Iben (ed.), *Demokratie und Ethik wohin? Antworten auf die Globalisierung*, Münster 1998, 81–124.
3. J. F. Lyotard, *The Postmodern Condition. A Report on Knowledge*, Manchester 1986.
4. See H. Peukert, 'Zur Neubestimmung des Bildungsbegriffs', in M. A. Mayer and A. Reinarts (eds), *Bildungsgangdidaktik*, Opladen 1998, 17–29.
5. Cf. M. Gronemeyer, *Das Leben als letzte Gelegenheit*, Darmstadt 1993; also H. Kessler, *Das Stöhnen der Natur*, Düsseldorf 1990.
6. For what follows cf. H. Kessler, 'Das Natur- und Selbstverhältnis der Moderne', in id., *Ökologisches Weltethos im Dialog der Kulturen und Religionen*, Darmstadt 1996, 14ff.
7. Cf. e.g. C. Lash, *The Minimal Self: Psychic Survival in Troubled Times*, New York and London 1984; E. L. Deci and R. M. Ryan, *Intrinsic Motivation and Self-Determination in Human Behaviour*, New York 1985; G. Scherhorn, 'Die Unersättlichkeit der Bedürfnisse und der kalte Stern der Knappheit', in B. Biervert and M. Held (eds), *Das Naturverständnis der Ökonomik*, Frankfurt am Main 1994, 224–40.
8. R. Sennett, *Der flexible Mensch. Die Kultur des neuen Kapitalismus*, Berlin 1998.
9. Cf. J. Baudrillard, *Das perfekte Verbrechen*, Munich 1996, 215–23.
10. See H.-J. Höhn, 'Sinnsuche und Erlebnismarkt', *ThPrQ* 143, 1995, 336–71.
11. For an appearance by the Buddhist monk Lama-kartha in spring 1999, St Peter's Chruch in Frankfurt was filled with people, each of whom had paid DM29 to enter and who listened to his chanted meditation for an hour. Asked at the end what they had found here, assuming that they did not understand the Tibetan songs, their replies were: 'The text wasn't important; it was the mood, the radiance, the spiritual: it was a quite special experience.'
12. See C. Duquoc, 'Christian Faith and Cultural Amnesia', *Concilium* 1999/1, 101–6.
13. Augustine, *Confessions* I, 1.
14. B. Pascal, *Pensées* 131, 164, 425.
15. S. Kierkegaard, *Sickness unto Death* (1849); see E. Drewermann, *Strukturen des Bösen* 3, Paderborn 1978, 436–53.
16. G. Schulze, *Die Erlebnisgesellschaft*, Frankfurt am Main 1992, calls this 'fear of boredom' or 'missing out on knowledge', 'anxiety about missing something' (65).
17. E. Drewermann, 'Angst', *NHThG²*, 1991, I, 26 and 28. Similarly H. Kessler, *Erlösung als Befreiung*, Düsseldorf 1972, 37–40 and 87–95; E. Biser, *Überwindung der Lebensangst*, Munich 1995.
18. E.g. Meister Eckhardt, *Deutsche Predigten und Traktate*, Munich 1943: God wants to have this temple, namely us, 'empty, so that he can be in it and find room in us with his love – which does not seek its own'. Therefore we must 'become free from the tie to the self and ignorance' (153ff.) in order to 'take leave of and die to all things'; we will rediscover them and ourselves complete in God (326).

19. See H. Kessler, 'Partikularität und Universalität Jesu Christi. Zur Herme-neutik und Kriteriologie kontextueller Christologie', in R. Schwager (ed.), *Relati-vierung der Wahrheit? Kontextuelle Christologie auf dem Prüfstand*, Freiburg 1998, 106–55: 133–8.

20. This is how H. W. Schumann, *Buddhismus. Stifter, Schulen und Systeme*, Olten 1975, 100, or slightly altered in the new edition (Munich ²1993), 108f., describes the Buddhist goodness (*metta*) of all being; it has the 'purpose of removing the hatred from one's own heart'; it serves one's own cleansing and redemption, whereas 'the object of the goodness is of subordinate importance'.

21. For a more detailed discussion see Kessler, *Überwindung als Befreiung* (n. 17), 37–40, 87–95, and id., *Christologie. Handbuch der Dogmatik*, Düsseldorf 1992, 239–442, here 392–409.

22. See A. Biesinger, *Kinder nicht um Gott betrügen*, Freiburg 1994.

Documentation

The Success of 'The Experience Society' and the Most Obvious Mistakes in its Reception

Götz Lechner

I. Gerhard Schulze and success

Gerhard Schulze's *magnum opus Die Erlebnisgesellschaft* ('The Experience Society') was widely praised after its appearance in 1992. 'The results arrived at . . . both theoretically and empirically, can be regarded as a real challenge to the traditional theory of classes and strata' (Honneth 1992, 524). '. . . With *The Experience Society* Gerhard Schulze has succeeded in a great venture which will hold the attention of the sociology of culture' (Müller 1993, 760). 'Schulze's brilliant work, the perspective, detail and rich thought of which is beyond any review, is a shining light' (Bambach 1993, 367). 'With his carefully researched and perceptively interpreted investigation Schulze gives the reader more than just access to the changed social and cultural structure of our society' (Fromme 1995, 150). 'Without doubt Gerhard Schulze is highly successful in his work . . . Schulze takes a good deal of time to develop and present his theses in a detailed and knowledgeable way' (Eckert and Jacob 1994, 131). All these evaluations come from reviews in which, particularly in the sphere of the educational sciences, the volume of discussions of Schulze's *The Experience Society* is overwhelming. In addition, no investigation which has appeared in German and which has 'life-style' in the title has failed to discuss Schulze (cf. Glocke 1993, Herlin, Scheller and Teplin 1994, Ritter 1997, Konietzka 1995 and Spellerberg 1996).

The most recent success in the triumphal history of *The Experience Society* is the use of its typology of milieus of experience in professional market research (cf. Jakob 1998) – however, here not much of the basic theoretical foundation remained.

II. *The Experience Society* and a series of misunderstandings

1. The beautiful experience and the change in values

If the reception of *The Experience Society* in this context mostly turns on the description of the structure given here, the extra-disciplinary references are anchored in the concept of the beautiful experience, the striking part of the title of this investigation. Whether in philosophical examinations (cf. Welsch 1996) or in politological (cf. Lindskoog 1995) or psychological dissertations (cf. Maase 1994), the concept of experience stands in the foreground. Here its scope is usually overestimated. A beautiful experience need not necessarily be youthful and hedonistic; in some circles a beautiful experience will have its place specifically in the pressures of a traditional value orientation. As an example one might cite the 'experience paradigm' of the social aggregate which Schulze has baptized the 'niveau milieu':

> The experience paradigm is the vision of the granting of the Nobel Prize: to the standing ovation of the international public the prize-winner walks to the dais, modestly, but far exalted above the public acclamation, since he is obligated only to one value, the highest, namely truth' (Schulze 1992, 287).

This leads to the second fundamental misunderstanding in the reception of Gerhard Schulze's work: the perception of the experience society as a diagnosis of a change of values.

Certainly at a methodologically abstract level Schulze's experience society can be given a place in a long series of diagnoses of the time with a sociological orientation. If we follow Reese-Schäfer (cf. Reese-Schäfer 1996, 379ff.), this series begins with Riesman (1950) and leads through Schelsky, *Die skeptische Generation* (1957), and Gehlen, *Die Seele im technischen Zeitalter* (1957), to Inglehard, Ulrich Beck (1986) and Gerhard Schulze. Alongside this orientation on social psychology, Schulze's reception by scholars as a theoretician of the milieu and life-style may be responsible for his acceptance into the circles of those who research changes in value, but prominent studies in this sphere (here one might think of Nowak and Becker or Glukowski) depict the structure of the milieu in a cross of co-ordinates of material and post-material values and stratification. To the same degree, the much-acclaimed change in values in not Schulze's theme – in his comprehensive set of questions there is not a single item from the current investigation of values. In terms of the sociology of culture Schulze's attention is focussed on the modern phenomenon of the removal of boundaries; he is concerned with the phenomenon of the consumption of culture in a consumer culture. Behind this consumption of culture, according to Schulze, we have no more and no less than a new model of social integration. But there is a series.

> The removal of boundaries is the most general formula to which the change of everyday life since the end of the war can be reduced. In the last thirty years real income has risen fourfold, the level of saving eightfold, incomes sixteenfold. The offer of goods and services has become infinite. The history of say a drug store, a car dealer or tourism represents a single headlong process of the diversification of what people can do without (Schulze 1993, 406).

The removal of frontiers thus means an increase in the possibilities. Now, however, this relates not only to opportunities of consumption in supply and demand; living arrangements are attaining a range of choice which is unique in social history. Schulze's notion of the removal of boundaries is not covered by the reservations over prosperity expressed in exemplary fashion by Claudia Ritter (cf. Ritter 1997, 49). In her view the origin and continuation of the formation of life-style is the consequence of the development of material prosperity and – with qualifications – a rise in living standards. For Schulze, the removal of boundaries is a 'phenomenon of modernization which will not be driven away even by unemployment, recession and a stagnation in real income' (Schulze 1993, 407). The removal of frontiers changes the relationship between subject and situation. 'If the boundaries of a situation are drawn narrowly, an attempt will be made to influence the situation. With the expansion of possibilities this kind of action retreats; the place of influence is taken by choice as a type of action' (Schulze 1993, 407ff.). Schulze's definition of an experience society is a social world now characterized by the way in which the social setting of the individual makes actions possible rather than restricting them, which sets a choice from the possibilities of the world above the influence on the limitations that this world represents for the individual. In the relativizations of the last sentence we already detect the scope of this morphological diagnosis of society: contrary to all the over-interpretation of this term which has come about in the meantime,

Schulze understands the topic of the 'experience society' to be one of a process. Moreover, here he is referring to the 'old' Federal Republic of Germany.

If classical, simple modernity, as Beck calls it, was a modernity of purposive rationality, now a rationality of experience predominates in this experience society.

As Eckert and Jakob (cf. Eckert and Jakob 1994, 131) aptly note, Schulze here overcomes the reification of the scheme of categories in an expressive instrumental way, as it seized on the conceptual systems of Max Weber and Talcott Parsons: rational action does not necessarily relate to the overcoming of external situations; it also relates to the production of inner states. In Schulze's terms, action orientated on experience has an inner focus: 'It relates to goals in ourselves: feeling, psycho-physical process, experiences' (Schulze 1993, 409). Action with an inner focus is no longer concerned with coping with life; rather, the goal is the project of the beautiful life, and it is here that the harshest differences from current negotiations in the change of values lie. As has already been said, the beautiful life can also be found in a traditional framework.

Now we have got so far, it is time to quote from the around twenty lines which Schulze devotes to the discussion of a change off values in his *magnum opus*:

> A change of values, post-materialism, individualization: the abundance of work suggests . . . two assumptions which were important for this investigation: first the thesis of an increase in inner orientation, and secondly the thesis that this development is sparked of by the multiplication of possibilities (Schulze 1992, 87).

Does the delimiting of the subject, the increase in inner order in society, now lead to the end of the social, to social atomizing? In particular Ulrich Beck's theory of individualization, which begins from similar premises to those of Schulze, is frequently and not inappropriately confronted with this criticism (cf. Hörning, Gerhard and Michailow 1990). Schulze counters what he thinks to be the 'error of individualizing' (Schulze 1992, 415) by stating that beautiful experiences are prone to disappointment and thus need a collective framework to safeguard them and ultimately to make them reliable. Gehlen is mentioned in support of this argument. Honneth, whom I go on to quote (Honneth 1992, 524), sums them up most clearly.

If individual action was directed only towards this goal of the heightening of personal experience, the subject would get into a spiral of self-observation which would irresistibly lead to circumstances of disappointment and uncertainty. For with ever-renewed fulfilment of the wish for experience there grows not only the danger of a fading in the attraction of satisfaction but also uncertainty as to how one's own wishes and tendencies are in fact made. Therefore the subjects, in order to counter both dangers, develop an inner readiness both for the formation of individual custom and also for the attachment to social groups. The first mechanism for ordering experience extracts from the flood of possible attractions of experience a mass of stable wishes and purposes that can be coped with; through the second mechanism of ordering, wishes for experience capitalized in this way are stabilized in interchange with interactive partners of the same mind.

If we follow this argument, it is obvious that individualization in interplay with an orientation on experience cannot lead to the atomizing of society.

The stabilizing exchange with others is made possible by 'sign groups of equivalent significance' – in Schulze's terminology 'everyday aesthetic schemes', which are canonized in a way that encompasses society by means of verdicts of similarity.

Everyday aesthetic schemes, the scheme of triviality, tension and high culture, form as it were the material for the constitution of social milieus. Primarily in terms of the sociology of knowledge, but also at the level of psychological measurements of attitude, Schulze assigns a level of meaning to these everyday aesthetic schemes: this is composed of the elements of genus, distinction and a philosophy of life. The abstract level of meaning manifests itself in the everyday aesthetic praxis of five typical major groups: the milieus of entertainment, self-realization, integration, harmony and level. For Schulze, milieus are groups of persons who stand out from one another by forms of existence which are specific to groups and enhanced communication within them. These forms of existence can make use of the sign repertoire of different everyday aesthetic schemes; they fuse the level of significance of these everyday aesthetic schemes with the normal definition of existential problems and a specific world-view within these milieus. In taking this step Schulze seems not only to abandon the idea of a unitary culture but in addition to state a 'decollectivization of models of reality' (Schulze 1992, 415). What Schulze means by this becomes clear if we compare it to a stratified society. Schulze attributes a marked collective consciousness to a class society which roughly corresponds to actual conditions. For contemporary society in the Federal Republic of Germany, it is of course true that there is still a superficial collective subdivision in which the majority of people have their place. However, the everyday sociological sense of this has declined (cf. Schulze 1992, 415). Schulze makes the declining perception of common features in the social situation, the milieu-specific particularization of criteria of prestige, the reduction of experiences of collectivity in the framework of conflicts between large groups, and the diminution of the 'we experience' which represents the milieu responsible for this (cf. Schulze 1992, 416). Nevertheless, notions of verticality within society have not disappeared, though they are present only in the form of split experiences of verticality. This is a split which manifests itself by generations. 'That nevertheless a milieu structure exists is connected with the experience market and those active in it: individuals seeking experience and co-operations offering it' (cf. Schulze 1992, 416). That brings us to the second fundamental misunderstanding in the reception of Schulze's work.

2. The experience society is like pregnancy: there isn't just a bit of it

The detachment of the individual from limiting structures is a well-known phenomenon in more recent sociological discussion. It can be referred to as 'disembedding' (cf. Giddens 1991). The isolation of the individual, a loss of reference, is always seen in an ambivalent way as an opportunity, but also as a risk: grasping life as liveable. Giddens again solves this problem in an individualistic way: isolation is broken through by two forms of trust on the part of the disembedded individual. This trust is, first, in the world (ontological security) and the functioning of this world, which is now thought of in technical terms: the functioning of expert systems, the functions of each of which can in turn be personalized. Secondly, it is trust in the other, with which a relationship to trust in the world is restored. Trust removes burdens, yet nevertheless isolation remains a typical phenomena of modernity: the individual is occupied with the project of the self. We find a similar pattern of argumentation in Schulze only for parts of the milieu system. As we have already seen, Beck (1983, 1986) understands the process of individualization more radically his pragmatic article 'Beyond Rank and Class'. If we follow his notion of the detachment of the individual from traditional rank and class relationships, along with the mentalities that go with them, and the collective unburdening that results, we necessarily end up with an atomized society, a society of isolated individuals. This makes the concept of society seem intrinsically questionable. Schulze sees the problem of the isolation of the individual as lying in the process of being detached from the limits of rank of class. However, he comes to the conclusion that 'society' will become anything but obsolete. The concept of society is not in process of disappearing but needs reinterpretation. Giddens' programmatic postulate 'neither system nor social integration', which was connected with the duality of structure, is resolved here in an interesting way. Schulze launches a pincer attack on the old conceptual division of system and social integration, since Lockwood also the micro-macro dichonomy, from two sides. By means of the construct of orientation on experience and the further concept of rationality of experience Schulze argues from the individual through social interaction to system integration, from taste societies to taste provinces (milieu), which people know to be different. And precisely this difference also serves to legitimate the way one is here and now. Distinction here, though, does not mean the consolidation of an economic status, as it does for Bourdieu; merely an aesthetic dividing line divides the milieu. These provinces of taste go beyond Zygmunt Bauman's 'tribe'; they are simply more comprehensive and make possible a division and perception of the world which recognizes similarities and inferences in a whole which can still be distant, alien and threatening to the 'neotribalists' in Bauman's building.

The commandeering of the market in experience markets also attacks these milieus which are difficult to think of in particularistic, post-modern terms. Here Schulze argues from system integration in the direction of social integration. A strong similarity to Simmel can be detected in the structure of the argument: it is about reciprocal relationships, not about causal hierarchical derivations.

The normative culture of present-day society no longer derives from the problem of maintaining a biologically probable time of life, building and existence and surviving the fight for existence generally. For all the consciousness of crisis, life is regarded as guaranteed. The important thing is to spend it in a way which one feels to be worthwhile. The core problem that now structures everyday experience is not life in itself but pleasure in it. Uncertainty is part of this problem. What do I really want? (ibid., 60).

So if an orientation on experience is the core of the normative culture of present-day society, among other things, with the problem of uncertainty the question arises what is worth striving for and what guarantees a beautiful experience. In addition to this uncertainty there is the risk of disappointment, however, as has already been shown. 'Unburdening is brought about by schematization' (cf. ibid. 203). Schematizations manifest themselves in personal style, and here Schulze brings in a second guarantor, namely Simmel:

> If we follow Simmel (1908), this personal tie to collectivity in the style practised is not an element which is disappearing but one that is arising in modernity, which promises support in the groundlessness of subjectivism (ibid., 187).

The quest for the beautiful experience thus on the one hand atomizes the world by making it subjective, and on the other, in order to complete this anthropological argument, introduces personal style, ultimately to exclude uncertainties, to minimize the risks of disappointment, schematizations and collectivizations of style. But the quest for the beautiful experience is only one side of the re-collectivized reality of Schulze's world-view. As I have already remarked, the other side is to be subsumed under the concept of 'commandeering the market'. On the market of experiences both the subjects as those seeking experience and those offering experience develop specific strategies to assimilate this constant relationship of intensification in the society orientated on experience.

> The rationality of the investigation of experience characteristic of our societies rests on the premise that one can bring about beautiful experiences by making the correct individual choices from a wealth of experiences on offer (ibid., 431).

Schulze notes that the consumer of relational experiences generally ignores the two basic problems: uncertainty, and the risk of disappointment in seeking experiences. The important thing is to produce a beautiful experience, no matter what. Schulze mentions mechanisms of commandeering the market society, though these cannot be assessed adequately here (cf. ibid., 432ff.). They make one thing above all clear: experience societies can exist only where the 'functional' product's usefulness is unquestionable and the whole market event is orientated on the additional usefulness of the quality of experience. It is this which raises the typical problem of orientation in the 'experience society', a problem which differs from the typical upper-class problem of the fight against boredom (Veblen is the classic account here) to the degree that not fashions, but only particular foundations for meaning appear as the way out.

III. Summary

Gerhard Schulze's *The Experience Society* is and has been extremely successful. Now in a seventh edition, it has found and still finds a generally positive reception far beyond the bound of its discipline. That may be above all because of the title, which seems to hit on one of the semantic cores of modern industrial societies: in a hedonistic world, at the end of all values only individual satisfaction in the form of a beautiful experience counts. One can put the label 'experience society' on this interpretation, but it is not covered by Schulze's theoretical and empirical efforts, as has been shown in this article. These over-interpretations and false interpretations do not do justice to the complexity of Schulze's work. In a distinctive terminology, with concepts of differing scope, the author, basing himself methodologically on possibly the most difficult to understand of German sociologists of the generation of the founding fathers, namely Simmel, has produced a dense work of great compactness at the cost of a lack of connection with other theoretical schemes. This is also one of the reasons why Schulze, with a few peripheral exceptions, is being read only in the German-speaking world: it is hard enough to penetrate this approach in an ancestral idiom. Thus there are hurdles before an appropriate translation of the work which deter publishers.

Translated by John Bowden

Select Bibliography

Bauman, Z. (1996), *Moderne und Ambivalenz*, Frankfurt am Main.

Becker, U., and Nowak, H. (1982), 'Lebensweltanalyse als neue Perspektive der Markt- und Meinungsforschung', *ESOMAR-Kongress*, Vol. 2, 247–67.

Bourdieu, P. (1992), *Die feinen Unterschiede: Kritik der gesellschaftlichen Urteilskraft*, Frankfurt am Main.

Eckert, R., and Jakob, R. (1994), 'Kultur- oder Freizeitsoziologie? Fragen an Gerhard Schulze', *Soziologische Revue* 7, 1994, 131–8.

Fromme, J. (1995), 'Gerhard Schulze: Die Erlebnisgesellschaft. Kultursoziologie der Gegenwart', *ZfP* 1, 1995, 146–50.

Giddens, A. (1984), *The Constitution of Society: Outline of the Theory of Structuration*, London and New York.

Giddens, A. (1990), *The Consequences of Modernity*, Oxford and Stanford, CA.

Giddens, A. (1991), *Self-Identity and Modernity*, London.

Honneth, A. (1992), 'Soziologie, eine Kolumne. Ästhetisierung der Lebenswelt', *Merkur* 6, 1992, 522–6.

Linskoog (1995), 'Sociologins objekt eller politikens begrepp? Reflektioner kring begreppt "civilt samhälle" ', *Sociologisk forskning* 32.1, 1995, 24–30.

Jakob, E. (1998), 'Marken-Milieus: Zwischen Harmonie und Niveau', *Media und Marketing* 8–9, 1998, 72–4.

Maase, K. (1994), 'Spiel ohne Grenzen', *Zeitschrift für Volkskunde* 90, 1994, 13–16.

Reese-Schääfer, W. (1996), 'Zeitdiagnose als wissenschaftliche Aufgabe', *Berl. J. Sozl* 3, 1996, 377–90.

Ritter, C. (1997), *Lebensstile und Politik*, Opladen.

Müller, H. P. (1993), 'Gerhard Schulze: Die Erlebnisgesellschaft. Kultursoziologie der Gegenwart', *KZFSS* 4, 1993, 778–80.

Schulze, G. (1992), *Die Erlebnisgesellschaft. Kultursoziologie der Gegenwart*, Frankfurt am Main.

Schulze, G. (1993), 'Entgrenzung und Innenorientierung. Eine Einführung in die Theorie der Erlebnisgesellschaft', *Gegenwartskunde* 4, 1993, 405–20.

Simmel, G. (1988). 'Die Arbeitsteilung als Ursache für das Auseinandertreten der subjektiven und der objektiven Kultur', in Dahme, H.-J., and Rammstedt, O. (eds) (1988), 95–128.

Spellerberg, A. (1996), *Soziale Differenzierung durch Lebensstile. Eine empirische Untersuchung zur Lebensqualität in West- und Ostdeutschland*. Berlin.

Welsch, W. (1996), 'Aestheticization Processes', *TCS* 13.1, 1996, 1–24.

Contributors

Zygmunt Bauman is Emeritus Professor of Sociology of the Universities of Leeds and Warsaw. His most recent publications are: *Globalization: The Human Consequences*, and *Work, Consumerism and the New Poor* (both 1998).

Address: 1 Lawnswood Gardens, Leeds LS16 6HF, UK.

John Joseph Puthenkalam, SJ, was born in Kerala, India, in 1956. He joined the Society of Jesus in 1976. After taking degrees in philosophy and economics, in 1986 he went to Japan. He did his theology studies in Sophia University. During 1993–1996, he was at the University of Glasgow, where he obtained his doctoral degree in economics. He taught at Ateneo de Manila University, the East Asian Pastoral Institute, and Maryhill School of Theology, in the Philippines. Presently, he is an Associate Professor in the Faculty of Humanities, at Sophia University, Tokyo. He is the author of many articles and of *The Comprehension of Freedom: Eastern and Western Ways of Thinking* (1995), and *Integrating Freedom, Democracy and Human Rights into Theories of Economic Growth* (1998).

Address: SJ House 7–1 Kioicho, Chiyoda-ku, Tokyo, 102–8571, Japan.

Maria Clara Lucchetti Bingemer is married with three children. She teaches Systematic Theology at the Pontifical Catholic University of Rio de Janeiro, the Santa Ursula University and the Franciscan Institute in Petrópolis. She is working on a doctoral thesis at the Gregorian University in Rome. Her publications include: with Ivone Gebara, *Maria, mãe de Deus e mãe dos pobres* (1978; Eng. trans. *Mary, Mother of God and Mother of the Poor*, 1993); with J. B. Libanio, *Escatologia cristã* (1985, trans. into Spanish); 'Da teologia do laicato à teologia do Batismo — um ensaio para reflexão', in *Perspectiva Teológica* 19, 1987; in Spanish as

Páginas, apart. no. 86); 'A Trinidade a partir da perspectiva da mulher', *REB* 46, 1986, 73–99. Her most recent work is *Jesuítas e leigos. Servidores da missao de Cristo* (1997).

Address: Rua Almirante Salgado 51, Laranjeiras, 22240–170 Rio de Janeiro RJ, Brazil.

MIKLÓS TOMKA was born in 1941; he studied economics and sociology in Budapest, Leuven and Leiden, and taught in Budapest, where he is now Professor of the Sociology of Religion. He has also been a visiting professor in Bamberg and Innsbruck. A co-founder of the Hungarian Pastoral Institute (in 1989), he is also Director of the Hungarian Catholic Social Academy and head of the Hungarian Religious Research Centre (both also from the same year).

Address: H–1171 Budapest, Vávix u.4, Hungary.

ALBERTO DA SILVA MOREIRA was born in Anápolis-GO, Brazil, in 1955. He studied philosophy and theology at the Franciscan Institute in Petrópolis and has worked with movements for the landless and with the Land Pastoral Commission (CPT) of the Catholic Church in Brazil. He gained his PhD at Münster University under the supervision of J.-B. Metz in 1988. Since 1991 he has lectured on Fundamental Theology at the St Francis University in Sao Paulo.

Address: Rua José Acedo Toro, 199, 12900–000 Bragança Paulista, SP, Brazil.
E-mail: amoreira@bragnet.com.br

FERDINAND DAGMANG was born in Davao City, Philippines, in 1954. He gained an MA in Theological Studies at Maryhill School of Theology, Quezon City, Philippines, and a PhD in Religious Studies at the Catholic University of Louvain on the ethics of liberation (focusing on the writings of Gustavo Gutiérrez). He currently teaches at the University of the Philippines, Diliman, Quezon City, Philippines and is engaged in research into popular religion.

Address: 70–B Olive St., SSS Village, Marikina City, Metro Manila, Philippines.

SUBHASH ANAND was born in Goa in 1943. He is Professor of Hindu Philosophy and Religion at Jnanadeep Vidyapeeth, Pune, has post-graduate degrees in Philosophy (1964), Theology (1968), and Sanskrit (1972), and a doctorate (1977) from the Benaras Hindu University, for his thesis on the Bhagavata-purana. He has written five books: *The Local Church and Inculturation* (1985); *Major Hindu Festivals: A Christian Appreciation* (1991); *Story as Theology: An Interpretative Study of Five Episodes from the Mahabharata* (1995); *The Way of Love: The Bhagavata Doctrine of Bhakti* (1995), and *Siva's Thousand Names: An Interpretative Study of Sivasahasranama* (1998), and numerous research articles. His main interest is to understand the contemporary significance of the rich Hindu narrative tradition and also to interpret the Christ mystery in the light of Hinduism.

Address: Papal Seminary, Pune 411014, India.

MICHAEL BONGARDT was born in Bonn and studied in Bonn and Munich. After ordination to the priesthood in 1985 he worked in a parish in Cologne. Between 1989 he worked at the Institute for Dogmatics and Theological Hermeneutics at the University of Münster, where he gained his doctorate in 1994 and his Habilitation in 1998. Since July 1998 he has been Dean of Studies at the Dormition Abbey, Jerusalem. He has written *Der Widerstand der Freiheit. Eine transzendentaldialog-ische Aneignung der Angstanalysen Kierkegaards*, Frankfurt 1995, and his Habilitationsschrift, *Die Fraglichkeit der Offenbarung. Ernst Cassirers Philosophie als Orientierung im Dialog der Religion*, will be published shortly.

Address: Kirchherrngasse 11, 28143 Münster, Germany.

NORBERT METTE was born in Barkhausen/Porta, Germany in 1946. After studying theology and sociology he gained a doctorate in theology, and since 1984 he has been Professor of Practical Theology at the University of Paderborn. He has written numerous works on pastoral theology and religious education, including: *Voraussetzungen christlicher Elementarerziehung*, Düsseldorf 1983; *Kirche auf dem Weg ins Jahr 2000* (with M. Blasberg-Kuhnke), Düsseldorf 1986; *Gemeindepraxis im Grundbegriffen* (with C. Bäumler), Munich and Düsseldorf 1987; *Auf der Seite der Unterdrückten? Theologie der Befreiung im Kontext Europas* (ed. with P. Eicher), Düsseldorf 1989; *Der Pastorale Notstand* (with O.

Fuchs et al.), Düsseldorf 1992; *Anstiftung zur Solidarität. Praktische Beispiele der Sozialpastoral* (with H. Steinkamp).

Address: Liebigweg 11a, D 48165 Münster, Germany.

DIANA L. HAYES is an Associate Professor of Systematic Theology at Georgetown University, Washington, DC, USA. Most of her work has been done in the area of liberation theologies in the United States, especially black and womanist theologies. She is the author of: *Hagar's Daughters: Womanist Ways of Being in the World*; *And Still We Rise: An Introduction to Black Liberation Theology*; and *Trouble Don't Last Always: Soul Prayers*. With Fr Cyprian Davis she is co-editor of *Taking Down Our Harps: Black Catholics in the United States*, and she has written numerous articles and book chapters. She has lectured throughout the United States and in Europe and South Africa. She is a member of the International Grail community.

Address: Georgetown University Theology Department, Box 571135, Washington DC 2DD57–1135, USA.

HANS KESSLER was born in 1938 and studied philosophy and theology in Tübingen and Würzburg. After gaining his diploma in Tübingen in 1961, he was engaged in pastoral work and religious education; he gained his doctorate in theology in Münster in 1969. Since 1972 he has been Professor of Systematic Theology at the University of Frankfurt am Main. His publications include: *Die theologische Bedeutung des Todes Jesu*, Düsseldorf ²1971; *Erlösung als Befreiung*, Düsseldorf 1972; *Sucht den Lebenden nicht bei den Toten. Die Auferstehung Jesu Christi*, Würzburg 1995; *Das Stöhnen der Natur. Plädoyer für Schöpfungsspiritualität*, Düsseldorf 1990; *Christologie: Handbuch der Dogmatik*, Düsseldorf 1992; *Ökologisches Weltethos im Dialog der Kulturen und Religionen*, Darmstadt 1996; and *Gott, der Kosmos und die Freiheit. Biologie, Philosophie und Theologie im Gesprach*, Würzburg 1996.

Address: Sodener Weg 43, D 65812 Bad Soden, Germany.

GÖTZ LECHNER was born in Marburg in 1994. He studied sociology at the University of Bamberg, where he gained a diploma. He has since been working as an assistant at the Technical University of Chemnitz. He is the author of a number of articles.

Address: Zietenstrasse 2, 09130 Chemnitz, Germany.
E-mail: goetz.lechner@phil.tu-chemnitz.de

The editors wish to thank the great number of colleagues who contributed in a most helpful way to the Final Project.

J. J. Alemany	Madrid	Spain
M. Althaus-Reid	Edinburgh	Scotland
J. Argüello	Managua	Nicaragua
G. Baum	Montreal	Canada
W. Beuken	Leuven	Belgium
T. Berger	Durham	America
V. J. Berkenbrock	Pétropolis	Brazil
A. Blijlevens	Heerlen	The Netherlands
F. Elizondo	Madrid	Spain
V. Elizondo	San Antonio	America
R. Gibellini	Brescia	Italy
F. Heselaars Hartono	Yogyakarta	Indonesia
M. E. Hunt	Tübingen	Germany
†B. van Iersel	Nijmegen	The Netherlands
O. John	Ibbenbüren	Germany
B. Kern	Mainz	Germany
U. King	Bristol	England
M. Klöckener	Fribourg	Switzerland
H. Laubach	Mainz	Germany
F. Magnis-Suseno	Jakarta	Indonesia
B. Mardiarmadja	Jakarta	Indonesia
F. W. Menne	Münster	Germany
J. M. de Mesa	Manila	Philippines
N. Mette	Münster	Germany
B. Metz	Münster	Germany
T. Michel	Rome	Italy
E. Pace	Padua	Italy
S. Painadath	Kerala	India
P. J. Philibert	Notre Dame	America
D. N. Power	Washington	America
M. Purwatma	Yogyakarta	Indonesia
G. Ruggieri	Catania	Italy
S. Ruiz	Chiapas	Mexico
A. Rizzi	Fiesole	Italy
P. Suess	Sao Paulo	Brazil
D. Singles	Lyon	France
E. Tamez	San José	Costa Rica
C. Theobald	Paris	France
M. Vidal	Madrid	Spain
F. Wilfred	Madras	India

CONCILIUM

Concilium 1990-1999

1990

1   On the Threshold of the Third Millennium   *The Concilium Foundation*
2   The Ethics of World Religions and Human Rights   *Hans Küng and Jürgen Moltmann*
3   Asking and Thanking   *Christian Duquoc and Casiano Floristan*
4   Collegiality put to the Test   *James Provost and Knut Walf*
5   Coping with Failure   *Norbert Greinacher and Norbert Mette*
6   1492-1992: The Voice of the Victims   *Leonardo Boff and Virgil Elizondo*

1991

1   The Bible and Its Readers   *Wim Beuken, Sean Freyne and Anton Weiler*
2   The Pastoral Care of the Sick   *Mary Collins and David Power*
3   Aging   *Lisa Sowle Cahill and Dietmar Mieth*
4   No Heaven without Earth   *Johann Baptist Metz and Edward Schillebeeckx*
5   *Rerum Novarum*: 100 Years of Catholic Social Teaching   *Gregory Baum and John Coleman*
6   The Special Nature of Women   *Anne Carr and Elisabeth Schüssler Fiorenza*

1992

1   Towards the African Synod   *Giuseppe Alberigo and Alphonse Ngindu Mushete*
2   The New Europe   *Norbert Greinacher and Norbert Mette*
3   Fundamentalism as an Ecumenical Challenge   *Hans Küng and Jürgen Moltmann*
4   Where is God?   *Christian Duquoc and Casiano Floristan*
5   The Tabu of Democracy in the Church   *James Provost and Knut Walf*
6   The Debate on Modernity   *Claude Geffré and Jean-Pierre Jossua*

1993

1   Messianism through History   *Wim Beuken and Anton Weiler*
2   Any Room for Christ in Asia?   *Leonardo Boff and Virgil Elizondo*
3   The Spectre of Mass Death   *David Power and Kabasele Lumbala*
4   Migrants and Refugees   *Dietmar Mieth and Lisa Sowle Cahill*
5   Reincarnation or Resurrection?   *Hermann Häring and Johann Baptist Metz*
6   Mass Media   *John Coleman and Miklós Tomka*

1994

1   Violence against Women   *Elisabeth Schüssler Fiorenza and Mary Shawn Copeland*
2   Christianity and Cultures   *Norbert Greinacher and Norbert Mette*
3   Islam: A Challenge for Christianity   *Hans Küng and Jürgen Moltmann*
4   Mysticism and the Institutional Crisis   *Christian Duquoc and Gustavo Gutiérrez*
5   Catholic Identity   *James Provost and Knut Walf*
6   Why Theology?   *Claude Geffré and Werner Jeanrond*

1995

1 The Bible as Cultural Heritage *Wim Beuken and Seán Freyne*
2 The Many Faces of the Divine *Hermann Häring and Johann Baptist Metz*
3 Liturgy and the Body *Louis-Marie Chauvet and François Kabasele Lumbala*
4 The Family *Lisa Sowle Cahill and Dietmar Mieth*
5 Poverty and Ecology *Leonardo Boff and Virgil Elizondo*
6 Religion and Nationalism *John Coleman and Miklós Tomka*

1996

1 Feminist Theology in Different Contexts *Elisabeth Schüssler Fiorenza and M. Shawn Copeland*
2 Little Children Suffer *Maureen Junker-Kenny and Norbert Mette*
3 Pentecostal Movements as an Ecumenical Challenge *Jürgen Moltmann and Karl-Josef Kuschel*
4 Pilgrimage *Virgil Elizondo and Seán Freyne*
5 From Life to Law *James Provost and Knut Walf*
6 The Holy Russian Church and Western Christianity *Giuseppe Alberigo and Oscar Beozzo*

1997

1 Who Do You Say That I Am? *Werner Jeanrond and Christoph Theobald*
2 Outside the Market No Salvation? *Dietmar Mieth and Marciano Vidal*
3 The Church in Fragments: Towards What Kind of Unity? *Giuseppe Ruggieri and Miklós Tomka*
4 Religion as a Source of Violence? *Wim Beuken and Karl-Josef Kuschel*
5 The Return of the Plague *José Oscar Beozzo and Virgil Elizondo*

1998

1 The Fascination of Evil *David Tracy and Hermann Häring*
2 The Ethics of Genetic Engineering *Maureen Junker-Kenny and Lisa Sowle Cahill*
3 Women's Sacred Scriptures *Kwok Pui-Lan and Elisabeth Schüssler Fiorenza*
4 Is the World Ending? *Sean Freyne and Nicholas Lash*
5 Illness and Healing *Louis-Marie Chauvet and Miklós Tomka*

1999

1 Unanswered Questions *Dietmar Mieth and Christoph Theobald*
2 Frontier Violations: The Beginnings of New Identities *Felix Wilfred and Oscar Beozzo*
3 The Non-Ordination of Women and the Politics of Power *Elisabeth Schüssler Fiorenza and Hermann Häring*
4 Faith in a Culture of Self-Gratification *Maureen Junker-Kenny and Miklós Tomka*
5 2000: Reality and Hope *Jon Sobrino and Virgil Elizondo*

Concilium Subscription Information - outside North America

Individual Annual Subscription (five issues): £25.00

Institution Annual Subscription (five issues): £35.00

Airmail subscriptions: add £10.00

Individual issues: £8.95 each

New subscribers please return this form:
for a two-year subscription, double the appropriate rate

(for individuals)   £25.00   (1/2 years)   . . . .

(for institutions)   £35.00   (1/2 years)   . . . .

Airmail postage
outside Europe +£10.00   (1/2 years)   . . . .

Total . . . .

I wish to subscribe for one/two years as an individual/institution
(delete as appropriate)

Name/Institution . . . .

Address . . . .

. . . .

. . . .

I enclose a cheque for . . . . payable to SCM Press Ltd

Please charge my Access/Visa/Mastercard no.   . . . .

Signature . . . . .Expiry Date . . . .

Please return this form to:
SCM PRESS LTD   9 - 17 St Albans Place   London   N1 0NX